D1203114

# A YANKEE *GUERRILLERO*

Brigadier General Frederick Funston at Vera Cruz while he was
Commanding Officer, 5th Reinforced Brigade (Army and Marines)
and Military Governor of the Mexican port city, April–November,
1914.

Courtesy of The Kansas State Historical Society, Topeka

# A YANKEE *GUERRILLERO*

Frederick Funston and The Cuban Insurrection

*1896-1897*

*THOMAS W. CROUCH*

MEMPHIS STATE UNIVERSITY PRESS

Copyright 1975 © by Memphis State University Press
All Rights Reserved.

No part of this book may be reproduced or utilized in any form or by any
means, electronic or mechanical, including photocopying and recording, or
by any information storage and retrieval system, without permission in
writing from the publisher.

Library of Congress Cataloging in Publication Data

Crouch, Thomas W        1932-
  A Yankee guerrillero.

  Includes bibliographical references.
    1. Funston, Frederick, 1865-1917.  2. Cuba—History
—Revolution, 1895-1898.  I. Title.
  F1786.F86C76      972.91'04'0924      75-20193
  ISBN 0-87870-027-7

# PREFACE

Recent events in Southeast Asia have placed the United States in the role of a counter-insurgency power. The military and naval forces of the United States have had to gear their operations to ferreting out and destroying units of communist irregulars who have been able to roam South Vietnam and adjacent states largely at will. Though the creation of the "Green Berets" has made all Americans cognizant of the nature of irregular warfare, there is much about guerrillas and their tactics that remains mysterious and distasteful to many people in the United States. Such feelings on the part of Americans are strange and inconsistent, since from the Revolutionary War onwards, Americans have often been "cheek by jowl" with guerrilla warfare. One has only to remember Francis Marion of the Revolutionary War and those who held out on Mindanao in the Philippines during World War II to grasp this fact of American military history.

Another episode during which Americans acted as guerrillas was the war in which the Cubans, for the second time in the nineteenth century, made a bid for independence from Spain. One of a score or so Americans who voluntarily went to Cuba and fought as a *guerrillero* was Frederick Funston of Kansas, an adventurous, courageous, and intelligent man who left us a record of his activities as a Cuban fighter.

By analyzing this record I hope to show the purposes and character of guerrilla warfare and describe how, from Funston's view, the Spanish might have contained it in Cuba. Besides, Frederick Funston was a *man*. He was a man whom all Americans should know, since he came from the heartland of the United States and reflected the philosophy and attitudes of that heartland at the turn of the century.

I have been assisted by many able and interested persons. Professor Joe B. Frantz, Department of History, The University of Texas (Austin) has been especially helpful. The entire staff of the *Kansas State Historical Society*, at Topeka, Kansas, in particular Robert W. Richmond, State Archivist, and Joseph W. Snell, Curator of Manuscripts, have given unstinting aid at every phase of the work.

I owe an especial debt of gratitude to my wife, Nancy Crouch, who has patiently spent much of her leisure time as historical critic, literary adviser, and typist.

Any errors of fact and interpretation that may be in the narrative must lie solely at my feet, for I am alone finally responsible for the view of Funston and the Cuban Insurrection herein contained.

Thomas W. Crouch
Memphis, Tennessee
March, 1975

# CONTENTS

KEY
1. HABANA
2. CAMAGUEY
3. NUEVITAS
4. GUAIMARO
5. LAS TUNAS
6. HOLGUIN
7. BANES
8. BAYAMO
9. MANZANILLO
10. GUANTANAMO BAY

SKETCH SHOWING LOCATION OF
FREDERICK FUNSTON'S ACTIVITIES
WITH THE CUBAN INSURRECTOS FROM
AUGUST 1896 TO DECEMBER 1897

# 1

## The Soldier and the Man

In the early years of the twentieth century, one of the more famous personalities in the United States was unquestionably Frederick Funston. An aggressive 120-pound, five-foot, four-inch Kansan, who sported a moustache and imperial beard, Funston was fast emerging as a real military hero to many North Americans. He had become an American soldier only in the spring of 1898. The governor of Kansas, recognizing the value of his fellow Kansan's recent combat experience with the Cuban *insurrectos*, appointed Funston colonel and commander of one of the volunteer regiments Kansas raised for the Spanish War.

Funston attracted national attention for his effective leadership of the 20th Kansas Volunteers during the regiment's days of training at San Francisco, California. Learning basic infantry drill and military regulations as he proceeded, Funston used pragmatic and colorful methods to initiate his volunteers into the military arts. He brought the regiment into fighting shape in amazingly short time. as the command occupied its seaside encampments during the summer and fall of 1898. Though he drove himself and his men hard, Funston was able to woo and win an Oakland belle for his bride before he sailed with his troops for the Philippines in October, 1898.

When the insurrection broke out on Luzon in early February, 1899, Funston won considerable acclaim. In April, 1899, during the first days of the northern drive of the United States forces toward Lingayen Gulf, he put a small force of his troops aboard a raft and led them across a broad stream in a maneuver that flanked the Filipinos' imposing defenses on the North bank of the *Rio Grande de la Pampanga*. Funston's move turned the enemy's formidable defense line at the *Rio Grande* and allowed Major General Arthur MacArthur's 2nd Division to continue its northward advance without significant delay. MacArthur's offensive, whose progress eventually caused the dissolution of the Filipinos' regular army in November, 1899, was a large step forward in the United States Army's extended campaign to pacify and subjugate the Filipinos. For his feat at the *Rio Grande,* Funston was awarded the Medal of Honor by President McKinley.

Though he returned with his Kansas regiment to the United States in the fall of 1899 for demobilization, Funston was by no means jaded with the life of a soldier. He was a national hero; shot in his left hand, he had shed his own blood for the American cause in the islands; and he held the impressive rank of Brigadier General of Volunteers. He was ready to go where the action was, and he longed to serve again as a soldier in the Philippines, where he believed history had thrust the duty of "civilizing" the natives upon the United States. So, he accepted the War Department's offer to go back to Luzon for a second tour of duty as a volunteer officer in December, 1899, and during the subsequent twenty-three months carried out his assignments with efficiency and verve.

The war in the islands had become a guerrilla conflict, but Funston was not long in making a name for himself as an excellent soldier in this type of combat. He became a most effective opponent of the Filipino guerrillas, whose tactics of terrorizing peaceful natives, raiding United States outposts, and ambushing army patrols had come to characterize the fighting on Luzon.

Funston excelled as a leader of counter-insurgency operations. He designed and led the daring scheme that effected the capture of Emilo Aguinaldo y Famy, the wary chieftain of the *insurrectos*. Aguinaldo had been covertly directing the guerrilla warfare against the Americans from his secluded hide-away in the forests of Northeast Luzon and was the best known hold-out against American rule. He was the key military figure of the insurgent movement that yet resisted the Americans by force. In late March, 1901, Funston and four other American officers, disguising themselves as enlisted prisoners of their loyal Filipino escorts who pretended to be guerrillas, made their way with much difficulty to Aguinaldo's remote headquarters. Funston and his dissembling expedition successfully seized the native leader alive in a celebrated *coup* that involved careful planning, good intelligence work, ability to endure hardship, and incredible good luck. Circumstances forced Funston, who, with his men, verged on starvation, to accept food from Aguinaldo, who had been completely deceived by Funston's elaborate, well-laid scheme.

While some Americans—including the famous author and critic Mark Twain—denounced Funston for the essential duplicity in the plan that undid Aguinaldo, most people back in the States deemed the capture of the Filipino leader to be an important stroke that did much to bring an end to the protracted guerrilla war in the islands. So believed the President and the War Department, for Funston, who was only thirty-six years old, and who, before 1898, had lacked any orthodox preparation as a soldier, received the rank of brigadier general in the regular army of the United States.

In the following years, Funston saw duty in various army stations in the Midwest and the West of the United States. In 1906, he served briefly and disappointingly in Cuba during the second intervention. One result of this short Cuban stint was that Funston became anathema to the then Secretary of War, William Howard Taft, whom President Theodore Roosevelt had given much of the responsibility for concluding a peace between the warring factions of the new island republic. By his own liberal interpretation of Taft's instructions and his desire to mediate effectively between the Cubans who were his old comrades-in-arms, Funston caused extra problems for Taft. As President, Taft consistently refused to promote Funston to the rank of major general.

During this same year Funston reclaimed much of the fame and respect that the Cuban episode had cost him when the catastrophic earthquake and fire struck San Francisco in April. Funston took command of relief and law enforcing activities for a time, though he did co-operate closely with local officials. Because of his initiative, Funston was responsible for heading off some of the potentially more tragic consequences of the disaster. Cut off from communication with the outside, he acted on his own, without the prior approval of either national or state authorities, and thus ran the risk of censure or worse for his well-meant, but decidedly authoritarian, actions. Most San Franciscans, however, looked upon him as the savior of their devastated city and continued throughout subsequent years to extol his name.

At Fort Leavenworth, Kansas, between 1908 and 1910, he acted as the commandant of the Army Service School, and he then returned to the Philippines for a third tour of duty. Funston was the commander of the Department of Luzon in 1911 and 1912, and he devoted much of his energy to training his command in intensive field maneuvers.

Throughout most of 1913, Funston was once more thrust by events into the center of a crisis situation. The War Department dispatched him to Honolulu, Territory of Hawaii, where his job was to improve the defenses in the vicinity of Pearl Harbor. The administration of President Woodrow Wilson was at that time undergoing a diplomatic crisis with the Japanese, and there was strong expectation in the War Department that the Japanese might carry out a sudden attack against the important Pacific naval base, should the strained relations lead to a Japanese-American war. Funston again did yeoman service, showing anew that emergencies only brought out the best in him. Fortunately, diplomacy removed the tension between the two nations, and Funston was freed to direct his attentions toward responsibilities in the American Southwest. There he did his most valuable work as a general officer of the United States army.

Funston's first responsibility along the Mexican border was to act as the military governer of the Mexican port of Vera Cruz from April to November, 1914. President Woodrow Wilson had ordered the navy to seize the city's dock facilities in order to prevent the government of Victoriano Huerta from receiving a shipment of arms, and staunch Mexican resistance had forced the marines and sailors to take the entire city in order to halt the shooting. The War Department then sent Funston to consolidate the conquest and to govern it till the two governments could reach an agreement. He was to avoid further fighting if at all possible.

To the astonishment of many of his army colleagues and countrymen, Funston, whose reputation was that of the combative, fighting "Bantam of the Army," kept the peace at Vera Cruz. In spite of the tense situation and the many provocations that his men faced, he was the model of restraint and caution. Not only did he strictly follow the orders of the President to avoid commencing hostilities that would have probably led to a second Mexican-American war, but he also governed the port city in an enlightened way. When the occupation ended, Funston received his long-awaited elevation to the rank of major general. At this point, he was ready for his most significant contribution as an American soldier.

In February, 1915, Major General Frederick Funston, who was now one of the five highest ranking officers on active duty with the United States Army, became the commander of the Southern Department. This command was probably the toughest post in the purview of the War Department. The Southern Department's confines ran from Brownsville, Texas, to Yuma, Arizona, and its main task was the protection of this vast border area from the violence that had been spawned by the numerous repercussions of the Mexican Revolution.

In spite of the myriad problems—military, diplomatic, and civilian—that this command slot entailed, Funston did a fine job. His reputation in the Southwest on both sides of the border was that of an energetic leader who always took action in a dramatic way; he was direct and forceful, and though he was sometimes quick to anger and often outspoken, he was always fair and approachable. The Texans highly esteemed him and referred to him with fondness as "The Little Guy." The Mexicans out of rueful admiration referred to him as *"El Chiquito Diablo."*

The work of commanding the immense and complicated Southern Department exacted a huge toll on Funston's physical stamina. Though he was only in his early fifties, he had developed a heart condition, and his sturdy constitution withered under the strains of his post. On February 19, 1917, he suddenly died of a heart attack while he sat in the lobby of San Antonio's St. Anthony Hotel, and the whole nation was almost as grief-stricken as his widow, son, and two young daughters.

Funston's body lay in state in San Antonio's *Alamo*, a sure sign of the Texans' respect for him. The funeral train that moved his remains to San Francisco for burial in the *Presidio* was met by civilian and military groups who did him last honors all along the route. Now that war with Germany loomed on the horizon, all Americans realized that the nation's army would surely miss the fighting talents of Frederick Funston, who had been one of the most effective soldiers in American military history.

Fortunately, Brigadier General John J. Pershing, Funston's subordinate who had just returned from successfully leading the Punitive Expedition into Mexico to quell the forces of Francisco "Pancho" Villa, was at hand to step into the vacated command post of the Southern Department. In due course, Pershing rose to the command of the American Expeditionary Force, went to France, and wrote his own indelible page in American military history. But for his death at fifty-two, Frederick Funston would probably have commanded the A. E. F., and the American aspect of the history of the Western Front in 1917-1918 would have been somewhat different.

So, the question automatically arises: What were the factors that made a capable American military commander of Frederick Funston? The answer to this question is composed of two parts. Funston's personal background bestowed certain qualities that helped to make him an accomplished soldier, and at the proper time in his life, he took advantage of a chance to experience warfare at first-hand and discover that combat was his *forte* and soldiering his profession.

Frederick Funston had led an adventurous life for a long time before he became a soldier in the uniform of the United States. Born in New Carlisle, Ohio, on November 10, 1865, he was the son of E. H. Funston, a farmer and a battle-experienced Union Civil War veteran. However, Funston was brought to Iola, Allen County, Kansas, by his mother in 1867. A petite woman, who loved music and the finer things, she came to join her husband, who had earlier arrived and chosen a farm home for his wife, Frederick, and a newly-arrived second son. Thereafter, Iola's environs remained Frederick Funston's home until he attained his adult years. He grew up a farm boy, the eldest in a family of five sons and one daughter. Though his father entered Republican state and national politics, Funston did the usual farming chores and grew up as did his peers; he hunted in the nearby creeks and woods with his brothers and chums; he learned the lore and folkways of an area that was on the fringe of the Plains frontier; he was a part of a scene that was itself rapidly evolving from a farming frontier into a settled agricultural community. Also, Iola's area in the 1880's was coming to possess a degree of basic industrialization in the forms of cement manufacturing and oil and gas production.

A graduate of Iola High School, Funston tried his hand briefly at teaching in a rural elementary school. Ironically, he failed to score high enough on the competitive academic test that would have admitted him into the United States Military Academy at West Point. Somewhat disappointed, he belatedly entered the state university of Kansas at Lawrence. He remained about the Lawrence campus for a period of five years, although he never took his degree. He was an indifferent student, and he took more out of the extracurricular activities by far than he did his formal course work. Funston could be a good student when he so desired, but as a scholar, he preferred to emphasize his own independent reading, especially in the areas of romantic poetry, botany, and military and naval histories.

He made several life-long friendships at Lawrence, among them William Allen White, later the noted writer and journalist of Emporia, Kansas. He also enjoyed his comradeship with his brothers of the *Phi Delta Theta* fraternity, and he reveled in the pranks and jokes that made for him a campus-wide reputation as a likeable and companionable young man.

Funston's distinction also stemmed from something else. He seemed to have an insatiable appetite for adventure and an ingrained restlessness that along with financial considerations caused him to spend alternate semesters away from Lawrence working at various jobs. He was a short-lived journalist, and he worked as a ticket-taker for the *Atchison, Topeka, and Sante Fe Railway.*

He always seemed to be able to make a rather humdrum job a source of excitement. He did the same on the summertime camp-outs that he took in Colorado's mountains with his college chums. Where Frederick Funston went, there was humor, excitement, and adventure. Funston loved events that stressed physical endurance, courage, and resourcefulness.

As his college friends struck out into the world to become academicians, lawyers, writers, and in some cases, politicians, Funston hit upon his first career. He became adventurer-explorer-field botanist all rolled into one. Through the efforts of his father and his keen long-time interest in botany, he landed a spot on an expedition that the Division of Botany of the United States Department of Agriculture was sending into the Dakotas during the summer of 1890 to collect grass specimens. He did such good work as a field man that the Department's botanists called on him the following year when they made up the personnel lists for a much more important and demanding expedition.

The area that the Department was going to study botanically and geologically in 1891 was Death Valley, the dreaded desert depression that lay both in California and Nevada. Funston worked directly under the young botanist Frederick Vernon Coville, who in later years became one of the world's recognized authorities on desert plant life and made lasting contributions in this area of the natural sciences. Coville's expedition suffered many hardships because of the extreme harshness of Death Valley's climate, and during the almost nine months that the group remained in the furnace-like region's confines, Funston came close to losing his life on several occasions. However, he triumphed over the tough physical conditions that he had to face. He had proved his worth as a resourceful field man, and the Department's scientific brains remembered him when they envisioned an even more ambitious field project.

The Department's plans now sent Funston northward to the Territory of Alaska, where, during 1892, 1893, 1894, he carried out two separate scientific field expeditions for the Division of Botany. His mission on each journey was to make a survey of the plant life, collect specimens of botanical growth, and write a general narrative of the features of terrain and climate that he thought to be significant. Funston made good his commission, and, in doing so, he contributed important botanic and geographical information to the authorities in Washington, D.C., about the nation's northernmost possession.

The first expedition took up only the summer of 1892. The Alaskan area that Funston visited was that of Yakutat Bay, a watery indentation of the Alaskan coastal "panhandle" that lay near the foot of towering Mt. McKinley. Aided only by a handyman, whom he had hired in Seattle, Funston explored all the fringes of Yakutat Bay. He traveled often by Indian canoe, pushing up glacier-lined inlets and then going ashore and tramping up the wooded slopes as far as the icy timberline near the snowcaps in order to take a full array of the indigenous plant samples. In spite of an unusually heavy summer rainfall, he perservered. He succeeded in gathering, drying, and pressing numerous plants that he took to Coville and the other scientists who were awaiting his return in the national capital.

During 1893 and 1894 Funston embarked alone

into the interior of Alaska. He was undertaking a much more ambitious expedition for the Department of Agriculture than the one that he had carried out during the previous year. While he was to do his usual botanical collecting and make his geographical observations, Funston was to go by an assigned route that was a formidable one indeed. The Kansan was to traverse down the upper Yukon River to its confluence with the Porcupine, a stream that flowed from the Northeast and originated above the Arctic Circle. He was then to course up the Porcupine to a point that lay just above the Arctic Circle, where he was to winter. In the spring he was to retrace his path to the Yukon and follow that stream to the Bering Sea, where he would contact a Coast Guard cutter and begin his return to the United States.

Funston carried out his instructions and then some. He met three prospectors on his voyage to Alaska, and since they were going his way, he went part of the way down the upper Yukon with them; then, he spent several weeks alone in the wilds not far from the Canadian boundary and about the miners' village known as "McQuestin's Post," where he took a large number of plant specimens; he then wintered above the Arctic Circle in accordance with his instructions, and made a remarkable snow-shoe trip in the dead of winter.

In the company of a few Indians, who were bartering pelts for trade goods, Funston made an exhausting tramp of nearly 200 miles, one way, and visited an isolated outpost of the Hudson's Bay Company that was set in the wilderness of Northwestern Canada. Before he began his return to the coast in the spring, Funston and an Indian companion trekked toward the Arctic Ocean. They linked up with a party of Indian hunters whom they encountered in the desolate tundra and tramped with them to the Arctic Ocean, striking it a few miles to the West of Hershel Island. There Funston visited with some Eskimoes; then, he chanced upon an ice-locked, American whaling fleet that was months out of San Francisco, and he eagerly renewed his social ties with his countrymen. After a few days' merriment, he returned to his lonely, snowbound cabin on the upper Porcupine, and a few weeks later, he began his return jaunt, moving alone down the Yukon toward the Bering Sea.

Funston had a brief brush with hostile Indians, and almost perished of loneliness. Although a capsizing of his boat in the lower Yukon caused him to lose many of his plant specimens and scores of the valuable photographs that he had made with his cumbersome camera equipment, Funston reached the coast safely. He was able to get back with many significant plant samples and added considerably to the scientific knowledge of North Americans about the topography of the Arctic Circle above the upper Porcupine. Funston had by this point developed an almost insatiable hunger for adventure, although he had understandably attained his fill of snowy scenes and Arctic solitude.

In 1894 after he had completed his official reports on his second Alaskan field expedition, Funston quit his government job and turned to a vastly different enterprise that was to take place in a totally different environment. He hatched the idea of setting up a coffee plantation either in southern Mexico or in Central America. To this end in late 1894 and early 1895 he gave lectures to Kansas audiences about his late Alaskan adventures, and he personally undertook a survey of properties along the Gulf coast of southern Mexico that might serve as a site for his plantation venture.

The trip to Mexico that consumed just about all of the Alaskan pay that he had accumulated was supposed to inform him about the currently existing conditions in the coffee-raising area. Armed with this first-hand knowledge, Funston believed that he could induce other entrepreneurs to enter into the scheme with him. Because of the impact of the "Panic of 1893" and upon advice of friends, Funston went to New York City in the latter half of 1895 in order to seek sources of capital. It was his intention to support himself by writing descriptions of his recent adventures and selling the articles to the big city's press and magazines.

At this point, the second factor that explained why Frederick Funston finally became a professional soldier in the United States Army became operative. While he was in New York City, Funston seized upon an opportunity to go to Cuba and fight with the Cuban insurgents against the Spaniards. It is this fortuitous event that this narrative seeks to describe. But, prior to such revelations, an estimation of what Funston's background had given him in terms of soldierly qualities and attitudes is in order.

Largely because of his Kansas upbringing, Funston had learned to exercise physical courage and aggressiveness successfully in spite of his diminutive size. He was loyal and companionable, and he was intellectually motivitated by a curious mind and a wish to learn for himself in his own way. He was a devout pragmatist, one who was bound neither by abstract theories nor by the "old ways" of doing things. He had learned to respect these qualities in others, and he was disdainful both of pretentiousness and timidity in others. He had little use for those who used their station in life to discourage questions, put down new ideas, and demand blind obedience.

Because of his family's community standing and his contacts at the University of Kansas, Funston epitomized the dominant North American values at the turn of the century. He was of the solid middle class, the segment of the population that furnished the leadership and fostered the ideology of the United States just when the nation undertook its "Big Mission" to acquire an exotic empire and "spread civilization" at the end of the

nineteenth century. He simply believed that his country's values—his class' values, really—were the best, and
he would strive earnestly to thrust them upon others
who were "backward," no matter how unwilling they
might be to accept them.

Before he could do his part of this "missionary
work" in the guise of a soldier, Funston had to go to
Cuba and participate in guerrilla warfare.[1]

---

[1] The author has based this summary of Funston's personality and career
mainly on his dissertation, *The Making of A Soldier: The Career of
Frederick Funston, 1865—1902*, The University of Texas (Austin), 1969;
he has also drawn broadly from two additional articles that he has written
about certain phases of Funston's interesting and many-sided life; see:
"Frederick Funston In Alaska, 1892—1894: Botany Above the Forty-
Ninth Parallel," *Journal of the West*, Volume X, Number 2, April, 1971,
pp. 273—306; and also, see: "The Funston-Gambrell Dispute: An Episode
in Military-Civilian Relations," *Military History of Texas and The Southwest*, Volume IX, Number 2, Spring, 1972, pp. 79-105.

# 2

## An Interest In Cuba

For Frederick Funston to give up on a cherished project was indeed out of the ordinary. The plan to set up a Mexican coffee plantation had absorbed Funston's thoughts and energies for several months. The venture as well had cost Funston his modest capital, and this money was a hard-won sum that Funston had accumulated by saving his Alaskan pay and by his lecturing on Alaska's wonders. Moreover, Funston was influenced by his friend and fellow Kansan, Charles S. Gleed of Lawrence. Under Gleed's persuasion, Funston concluded that eastern financiers might be more pliable than their poorer Kansas counterparts. The would-be entrepreneur accompanied attorney Gleed, whose business connections supposedly gave access to key banking circles, to New York City in March of 1895. Funston's aim simply was to borrow enough capital in order to revive his languishing tropical agricultural project.[1]

Funston found that the holders of American investment were even more cautious than usual. The reason was the depression of the 1890's. Because of the economic debacle that had been precipitated by the "Panic of 1893," no backers were forthcoming for Funston's

[1] Anonymous Newspaper Interview with E. H. Funston and Charles F. Scott at Iola, Kansas, F. Funston Papers, Box 75; "Notes on Frederick Funston by Eda B. Funston," F. Funston Papers, Box 76; all materials in the Frederick Funston Papers are held by the *Kansas State Historical Society* at Topeka, Kansas.

coffee-raising scheme. Before long, Funston's meager remaining funds were gone, and the Kansan had to find means to support himself. He did so only in order to prolong his stay in the metropolis. He still harbored the hope of eventually finding backers for his plantation.

Funston first tried living by his pen, and for several months he "was engaged in desultory literary work for the magazines and newspapers." Such an interlude was not surprising. Funston had the uncommon talent of being able to record his notable adventures in lean, lucid prose. Indeed, he had originally intended to raise at least a part of his capital in New York City by peddling his articles to the newspaper and magazine publishers.

There was something else important about Funston's ability as an author. It was through writing for a living that Funston manifested his first discernible interest in Cuba's revolt against the rule of Spain. He offered himself to the New York *Sun* as a war correspondent, but he was rejected by Chester S. Lord, the managing editor of the newspaper. Lord said that he did not believe Funston "would be of much use to the paper."[2]

Ironically, the depression eventually intervened to help Funston in his effort to remain in New York City just as it had earlier interfered to hurt him in his coffee enterprise. The *Atchison, Topeka, and Santa Fe Railway Company*, a business concern that was itself a victim of the hard times and an erstwhile employer of "ticket-taker" Funston, was undergoing a bankruptcy reorganization. This development necessitated the issuance of new securities. Gleed, whose commercial contacts extended into the troubled *Santa Fe* organization, knew of Funston's pecuniary difficulties. He influenced the di-

[2] Anonymous Newspaper Interview with E. H. Funston and Charles F. Scott at Iola, Kansas, *ibid.*; New York *Times Magazine*, February 25, 1917, pp. 1—2.

rectors to name his struggling friend to the temporary post of deputy comptroller. Though he understood the job would last only a few weeks, Funston gratefully took on the work during the spring of 1896. His main task was to issue the reorganized company's stocks and bonds, and his particular chore simply required him to sign his name "on each of several thousand bonds."

So it was that Funston, who in later times recalled his "writer's cramp," appended his signature to millions of dollars' worth of debentures that remained outstanding for years. There was little excitement in this dull routine. Funston tired quickly of this version of railroading and subsequently looked back on this employment with a kind of amused contempt. He told his friends that his:

> duty was to don a high hat and a Prince Albert coat every morning and go down to the Santa Fe executive offices. ...All ... [he] had to do in the morning was to sign ... [his] name to hundreds of bonds and stock certificates.
>
> At noon ... [he] maintained the dignity of ... [his] position by dining at the finest hotel in New York—on ... [his] expense account—and in the afternoon ... [he] returned to ... [his] sumptious office and signed ... [his] name a lot more.[3]

So Funston, in spite of his knowledge that this easy job would be short-lived, found the work unenjoyable. And, all the while, his chances at getting financial backing grew more and more remote. Things simply dragged

[3] F. F. Eckdall, "'Fighting' Fred Funston," Speech in *The Kansas Historical Quarterly*, Spring, 1956, p. 81; C. S. Gleed, "Romance and Reality," *Cosmopolitan*, July, 1899, pp. 326-327; "Persons in the Foreground: The Adventurous Career of Frederick Funston," *Current Opinion*, June, 1914, p. 428; Untitled Newspaper Article, Kansas City, Missouri, *Journal*, February 25, 1917, no page number, in *Frederick Funston, Clippings, Volume I, K.S.H.S.*; William Allen White, *Autobiography*, p. 306; the lengthy quotation above in which Funston described his job with the *Atchison, Topeka, and Santa Fe Railway Company* in the spring of 1896 came from the K. C. *Journal* article that was cited by this footnote.

too much to suit the ever-restless Funston. What happened next was therefore not surprising to any of Funston's friends. Before the summer was out Funston became interested in a project which was quite different from that of running a coffee plantation.

The new enterprise began with an innocuous stroll one evening in the spring. While he was sauntering along New York City's sidewalks, Funston found himself by sheer chance at Madison Square Garden. He noticed that a fair, an arrangement of the city's Cuban *junta*, a council of revolutionaries, was taking place. Filled with curiosity and with time heavy on his hands, Funston ventured inside the pavilion. Presently he observed that Cuban revolutionaries were staging the event in order to raise funds. He understood that all the money that they took in was ostensibly to be used by the *juntistas*, the members of the council, for the sole purpose of buying medical supplies for their homeland's *insurrectos*, the insurrectionists who were doing the actual fighting.

What Funston heard excited him far more than what he saw. General Daniel E. Sickles, an ardent Cuban sympathizer and colorful Civil War veteran, was occupying the speaker's rostrum. Sickles delivered a powerful, fire-eating speech in which he strongly praised the Cubans who were waging their fight for national independence. Had he been a hard-hitting evangelist who was bringing the word to a penitent backslider, the dashing and eloquent former Union officer could have not made a more convinced convert to his cause than he did with Funston. In just a few minutes, Sickles' remarks induced Funston to forswear all his plans and go to Cuba to fight with the *insurrectos*.[4]

---

[4] Frederick Funston, "To Cuba as a Filibuster," *Scribner's Magazine*, September, 1910, p. 305. Funston's Cuban and his Philippine Insurrection experiences appeared in book form in 1911 from the presses of Charles Scribner's Sons of New York. Bearing the title *Memories of Two Wars:*

Actually, the General's words acted more as a cata-
lyst than as a prime mover, because this decision was in
truth neither sudden nor surprising. Funston's coffee
enterprise had not materialized, and the routine of an
office job was indeed anathema to Funston. Always an
avid reader, Funston had followed the struggle in Cuba
from the outset. He had been from the first wholly on
the Cubans' side. He had concluded that the rebels'
cause was entirely equitable and that Spain's ineptitude
in colonial administration was sufficient reason to justi-
fy the curtailing of Spanish colonial power. Funston
sincerely thought that Cuba's history was a "pitiful
tale" in the annals of human society, because Spanish
colonial rule had been characterized by "brutality, corruption[,] and general cussedness."

Funston also justified his Cuban sympathies by idea-
listically linking the island revolt of the 1890's against
Spain with the rebellion that the thirteen North American colonies had waged against Great Britain a hundred
and twenty years earlier. The *junta's* struggle, so Funston hypothesized, was an extension of the aims of the
American revolt. It was a fight to abolish the remnants
of archaic thinking, feudal ways, and dynastic government in the New World. In a Social-Darwinistic vein, he
believed that the time was historically nigh for colonial
Cuba to change itself rapidly into a free, democratic
republic. Funston sanguinely thought that the islanders'
cause would triumph within six months, and that the
demise of Spain's colonial rule would be a natural and
healthy step down the road of progress. Hence, the

*Cuban and Philippine Experiences*, this book was based by Funston on the
series of articles that had appeared in *Scribner's Magazine* in late 1910 and
early 1911. Since the contents of the articles and the book are substan-
tially the same, the citations will use both sources interchangeably, refer-
ring to the book as: Funston, *Memories of Two Wars*.

Cubans' revolution was "the war of everyman who want . . . [ed] to take part in it."[5]

Although they were certainly ardent, these Darwinistic views did not by themselves explain Funston's decision to join the *insurrectos'* ranks. With his planting ambitions frustrated, Funston was considering another career as a journalist. Actually, he was anxious to make "some sort of [a] reputation" for himself in that field as a "war correspondent." After he had associated himself with the *junta*, he convinced the editors of *Harper's Weekly* to commission him as their reporter among the Cuban forces. This arrangement probably did something to strengthen Funston's resolve to go to Cuba, since he did not really expect the revolutionaries ever to be able to pay him for his military service. He looked to the magazine to credit him with a stipend for each article that he was able to get through to New York from Cuba. His earnestness in this enterprise was demonstrated by his including "a large camera" in his Cuban baggage. He wanted to be able to illustrate his articles appropriately and thereby enhance their worth to the publishers.

Even the potential of the Cuban struggle as a school for a budding war correspondent did not completely explain the strong appeal of Sickles' words to Funston. As was always the case when he determined to do something of import, Funston was moved by a consider-

[5] Armando Prats-Lerma, "La Actuacion del Teniente Coronel Frederick Funston (Norteamericano) en la Guerra de Independencia de 1895-1898," *Boletin del Ejercito*, Noviembre y Deciembre, 1931, pp. 361–362, F. Funston Papers, Microfilm 54, Number 4; hereafter this article will appear in the citations as : A. Prats-Lerma, "La Actuacion del Teniente Coronel Frederick Funston," *Boletin del Ejercito,* Nov.-Dec., 1931, p. *etc.*; C. S. Gleed, "Romance and Reality," *Cosmopolitan*, July, 1899, pp. 327, 330; Frederick Funston to Charles F. Scott, July 16, 1896, 361 West 57th St., New York City, New York, F. Funston Papers, Box 75; Frederick Funston, "To Cuba as a Filibuster," *ibid.*; William Allen White, "Gen. Frederick Funston," *Harper's Weekly*, May 20, 1899, p. 496.

able emotional factor. Underlying the decision to go to Cuba were both positive and negative psychological influences. On the positive side, Funston remained the incurable romantic whose lust for adventure, memories of his father's Civil War vignettes, and close reading of martial history and literature had bred in him a desire to experience actual combat. He truly wished "to see a real live war for . . . [his] own satisfaction." In a somewhat negative way, Funston was at loose ends; there was no alluring career in sight for him, and he still lacked either any "settled aim or clearly seen ambition." He was much chagrined by the failure of his coffee-raising plans, and he simply wished to go where he could "for a time get away from some of . . . [his] disappointments and bitterness against things in general."

Funston's personal scheme of things included no "ambition to get rich" in some mundane business line. He cared even less for any sort of political endeavor. All that he knew about his future in the summer of 1896 was that somehow he would "cut some ice in the world," and that he intended "to keep hustling" at something until his days were done. So, to Funston at this juncture, a righteous war seemed to offer the best avenue for his energies.[6]

Funston acted as though he had at last found his calling when he heard General Sickles' oration. On the day following the night of his visit to the Cubans' fair, Funston contacted the *junta*, who, *sub rosa*, of course, were always ready to recruit more volunteer fighters to

[6] Anonymous Newspaper Article, "Frederick Funston's General Career," F. Funston Papers, Box 75; Anonymous Newspaper Interview with E. H. Funston and Charles F. Scott at Iola, Kansas, F. Funston Papers, Box 75; Arthur Royal Joyce, Untitled and Uncited Article, October 29, 1917, F. Funston Papers, Box 75; Joyce was for a time one of Funston's fellow *expedicionarios* in Cuba; C. S. Gleed, *ibid.*; Frederick Funston to Charles F. Scott, July 16, 1896, *ibid.*; Frederick Funston, "To Cuba as a Filibuster," *ibid.*; William Allen White, *ibid.*

go to Cuba. Called *"expedicionarios"* by the Cubans, these volunteers were carefully scrutinized by the *junta* in order to weed out any hostile agents. Although he was cordially greeted by the rebel gentlemen, Funston recognized that his lack of credentials aroused suspicions. The *junta*, who were making a show of strict obedience to federal neutrality laws, alleged to Funston that they raised only funds, not men. This reticence did not deter Funston, who decided to overcome it by use of a friendly connection.

First Funston obtained a letter of introduction to General Sickles from a mutual acquaintance. Then he personally visited the maimed veteran and former diplomat and convinced him of his earnestness to serve the Cuban cause. As a result, Sickles wrote a letter in behalf of Funston to the proper Cuban circles. This influential missive went to certain New York City friends of the *junta* who arranged a meeting between the aspiring *expedicionario* from Kansas and a "Mr. Palma." This Cuban gentleman was Tomas Estrada Palma, who was a revolutionary leader and later the first President of the Cuban Republic.[7]

The outcome of the interview with Palma was successful. Funston learned that the *junta* would gladly accept his services. Yet, he had to go to Cuba before he officially joined the *insurrectos'* forces, because such a procedure would mean that the *junta* could continue to claim technically to be observing the tenets of United States neutrality. Until his departure, Funston understood that he would have to act with great prudence, and that his initial duties were quite simple. He would have to report once each week to the *junta*, and otherwise he would just have to bide his time patiently until the secret date of transit.

However, during one of these early weekly report-

---

[7] Frederick Funston, "To Cuba as a Filibuster," *ibid.*, p. 306.

ins, Funston received an assignment. A mysterious "Mr. Zayas," who was one of the *junta's* New York City agents, gave to Funston a task of a technical, military nature that was his first real work for the Cuban cause. Zayas discussed the Cubans' weakness in artillery with Funston and then told him that he could help to remedy this shortcoming. Funston found that he had something that both helped him to pass the time and to acquire a useful martial skill as well. Under Zayas' orders, Funston prepared to become an expert on field artillery for the *insurrectos*.

Funston began by taking a note of introduction from Zayas to the firm of *Hartley & Graham,* the arms dealers who were a regular supplier of the Cubans. The company's experts then introduced him to his new challenge—a Hotchkiss breech-loading cannon that fired a twelve-pound projectile. By carefully studying the instruction book and listening closely to the explanations of the manufacturers, Funston quickly learned to dismantle and manipulate this piece thoroughly. He committed to memory the tables of warhead velocities and ranges and soon became so knowledgeable a cannoneer that the pleased Zayas asked him to take on a second task. Funston agreed, and becoming an artillery instructor, he endeavored to pass along his recently-acquired knowledge of gunnery to a group of Cuban *juntistas*, who were also awaiting shipment to Cuba.

Funston's aptitude in learning about artillery on short notice is better understood when one remembers the state of development of field guns near the turn of the century. All of the guns that Funston handled in Cuba were relatively simple pieces, weighing less than 1,500 pounds or so, even when their crews had them fully assembled. All laying of guns on targets was done by the chief gunner—usually Funston—who used a direct-line-of-sight method that automatically precluded long-range, indirect fire. Because of aiming difficulties, this flat-trajectory fire was generally ineffective at ranges beyond 1,500 yards; so, much of Funston's artillery work was done by him within easy reach of the enemy's rifles.

All of these guns were disassembled by their crews who entrusted their transportation from battlefield to battlefield to pack animals. These animals also were the means by which Funston and his gunners attempted to keep themselves supplied with the ready-to-use, "fixed ammunition", or, "shells," that the manufacturer produced to accompany his gun. Almost all of this "fixed ammunition"—whose weight was heavy for its size—had to come from the United States, and, hence, it was difficult to obtain and was subjected to all sorts of deleterious factors by the rigors of its lengthy journey. *If* the "shells" got through the United States and Spanish coastal patrols, there was still the problem of corrosion by sea air to plague Funston and his cannoneers. Such corrosion could ruin "shells" and render them "duds," as could either improper, rough handling by teamsters or the dampness and rains of the Cuban interior.

Really, Funston's work as an artilleryman during the Cuban Insurrection, 1896—1897, was much the same as that of his father had been with the Union army during the Civil War in the United States. However, there were major differences—differences that reflected the changing "state of the art" and that revealed the on-going transition between the artillery technology of the mid-nineteenth century and that of the late years of the century. Unlike his father, Funston was operating "quick-firing" field guns. The bores were rifled; the ammunition was in one piece within a metal case that held the ignition system that "fired" the round, the charge that, upon detonation, propelled the "warhead," and the "warhead" itself.

In the guns of larger caliber that Funston handled—

the "12 pounders", pieces of 60–70 mm. bores, whose "warheads" weighed twelve pounds—the "warheads" contained internal trains of quick-burning, high-grade gunpowder that Funston could adjust by rotating a section of the "warhead" either clockwise or counter-clockwise. So, by manipulation, he could explode the missile either before its impact with a solid object or upon its impact with a solid object. These "fuzes" were especially sensitive to moisture and rough handling.

Funston's guns also differed from those that his father had served in that they were "breech loaders." That is, there were "blocks" at the rear of the barrels that admitted the "shell" into firing position in the chamber of the piece. The "shell's" metal case, held in place by the "block," helped to seal the chamber during firing, and a trigger device in the "block" detonated the "ignition system" in the rear of the "shell" and fired the round. There was also some crude type of recoil container on Funston's guns. Probably, there were interlocking metal plates—"slides"—some on the barrel and others on the wheeled undercarriage supporting the barrel that furnished this necessary mechanism and made it easier for Funston to lay the gun anew for the next firing.

Funston spent the remainder of the summer's nights until his departure for Cuba expounding the workings of the twelve-pounder for a group of about fifteen Cuban youths. The sessions met inside a closed room above a saloon. Situated "well up on Third Avenue," this establishment was a surprisingly safe site for Funston's illicit work. Neither New York state nor federal officials ever interfered with his training activities.

The authorities also appeared to be blind and deaf when, at one point, Funston attended a noisy artillery demonstration that involved the use of live ammunition in a brand-new Sims-Dudley dynamite gun. Held at a remote location on Long Island, the try-out of this unusual weapon released rounds of high-explosives that accidentally went off their mark. These shots exploded when they struck the ocean and raised geysers of water near a passing excursion boat. Fortunately, there were neither injuries nor damages, and no investigation ensued. So the artillery schooling continued.

Then, abruptly one afternoon in early August, 1896, Funston received his secret travelling orders. He was more than ready to leave. He had long since decided to ignore "some earnest protests from home and from [some] friends [who were] against this trip, . . . ." He was well prepared to take "some nasty chances" if the need arose, and he had concluded that he would just trust to his luck against "bullets and sich [sic]." He assembled his gear without delay, and, accompanied by J. Willis Gleed, who was the brother of Charles S. Gleed, he unobtrusively made his way to the *junta's* assembly place at the Cortlandt Street Ferry. He borrowed a small sum of money from Gleed, told him goodbye, and vanished by sunset.[8]

[8] Anonymous Newspaper Article, "Frederick Funston's General Career," F. Funston Papers, Box 75; C. S. Gleed, "Romance and Reality," *Cosmopolitan*, July, 1899, p. 327; Frederick Funston to Charles F. Scott, July 16, 1896, 361 West 57th St., New York City, New York, F. Funston Papers, Box 75; Frederick Funston, "To Cuba as a Filibuster," *ibid.*, pp. 306-308; John Batchelor and Ian Hogg, *Artillery*, pp. 2–22.

# 3

## The Furtive Transit

Funston naturally understood that his final destination was Cuba. However, he knew neither exactly how nor precisely when he would get there. He had learned for certain only that the delay in his starting was the result of "the non-delivery [by the manufacturer] of several of the Hotchkiss guns (little brown pets Kipling called them) . . ." These essential items were the pieces with which the newly-strengthened Cuban artillery unit was planning to fight. Everything else about his journey was shrouded in mystery.

Funston was taking part in a clandestine operation whose pattern had been well established by the *junta*. It was an endeavor whose magnitude constituted something of a record among its genre. Funston was part of the human contraband that composed the revolutionary expedition of Rafael Cabrera, whose cunning transfer of men and materiel to Cuba startled officials both in Madrid and Washington. Cabrera's expedition directly contributed to the growing estrangement between Spain and the United States over the matter of filibustering.

Of the seventy-one filibustering expeditions that emanated from covert Cuban bases in the United States between 1895 and 1898, the Spaniards intercepted only five, although they were finally employing a force of sixty-seven ships and over 200,000 soldiers to halt these forays. During the same interval, the avowedly neutral United States Government made use of naval, Coast Guard, and revenue vessels, as well as land-based officials of the Justice and Treasury Departments, to pre-

27

vent thirty-three of these excursions from getting through to their Cuban goals. Moreover, President Grover Cleveland's proclamations of December, 1895, and July, 1896, had promised stern punishment for any United States citizens who were caught by federal authorities either aiding, or transporting, or filibustering for the *insurrectos*.

These measures of the government of the United States did not satisfy the Spanish. They continued to denounce the activities of the *junta* on the mainland and called for its outright suppression by the national officials in Washington. In the light of these developments, the passage of Funston to Cuba with the expedition of Cabrera indeed demanded discretion. It was obvious to Funston that, while apprehension by the Spanish meant at least imprisonment for himself and death for the Cubans, apprehension by his fellow Americans would probably bring both a fine and incarceration down upon his neck and place the Cubans in a federal penitentiary. Either way, valuable manpower and materiel would be lost to the Cubans who were battling the Spaniards for their independence.[1]

Since they were well aware of these factors, the *junta* worked out an ingenious plan to avoid detection and apprehension of Cabrera's party by federal officers. This scheme involved the adroit use of southern railroads by Cabrera and his men and the dissembling deployment of seagoing vessels whose masters and crews were in the pay of Cuban revolutionaries. The key man in the railroad transportation was Alphonso Fritot, who was the joint agent for all the rail lines that had track connections running into Jacksonville, Florida. Fritot's

[1] "Frederick Funston," *Harper's Weekly*, March 5, 1898, p. 226; Frederick Funston to Charles F. Scott, July 16, 1896, 361 West 57th St., New York City, New York, F. Funston Papers, Box 75; R. V. Rickenbach, "Filibustering with the *Dauntless*," *The Florida Historical Quarterly*, April, 1950, p. 237; Samuel Proctor, "Filibustering Aboard *The Three Friends*," *Mid-America, An Historical Review*, April, 1956, p. 87.

main contribution was the authority that his job gave to him. He held the power to secure extra cars for passengers and freight at almost any time that he desired. His responsibility in the *junta's* plan was to provide the actual travelling accommodations for the *expedicionarios* who were undertaking their secret passage to their embarkation point on the southern Atlantic coast.

For the sea leg of the trip, the *junta*, who were more fearful than ever of a severe federal crackdown on their operations after Cleveland's second Proclamation, decided that they needed another ship. Accordingly they purchased the *Dauntless* at Brunswick, Georgia, for $30,000. Manned by a crew of seven, this three-year-old tugboat that reputedly was one of the fastest in the South could accommodate a cargo of seventy-six tons. Acting in the name of the firm of *Bisbeen & Foster,* who were building contractors of Jacksonville, Florida, and who also were operating a front organization for active Cuban sympathizers, Horatio S. Rubens dashed to Georgia and bought the vessel. Subsequently Rubens, who was attorney for the *junta*, took the *Dauntless* to Jacksonville, Florida, where merchant Jose A. Huau took possession of it. Huau, who was also a Cuban revolutionary agent, ran a town store that served as a clearing house for all of the filibustering operations in the Jacksonville Area.[2]

With the *Dauntless* purchased and deployed at Jacksonville by Rubens, the rebels were ready to begin their clever ruse. The heart of the deception on the sea involved the Cubans' leading the United States customs and coast guard officials to believe that the *junta* in-

[2] Rickenbach, *ibid.,* pp. 231-232. Rickenbach points out that by the time that Funston became a filibuster, tugboats were the mainstays of the *junta's sub-rosa* supply and replacement system that ran more or less regularly between the United States and Cuba. The sea-going tugs' ability to move speedily, jettison cargo quickly, and make a swift return to American waters made the Cuban revolutionaries highly prize these sturdy craft.

tended to make two expeditions with a pair of older and well-known filibustering vessels. These craft were really decoys. One was the steamer *Commodore*, a ship that was tied up at Charleston, South Carolina, and the other was the tug *Three Friends*, a vessel that was moored at a pier in Jacksonville, Florida. To achieve the necessary and crucial delusion, Rubens journeyed to Jacksonville and publicly conversed with the master of the *Three Friends*, whose crew subsequently commenced to take on coal.

In the meanwhile, Captain John "Dynamite" O'Brien, who was a notorious filibuster suspect and a tug master with much experience in Latin American waters, was also busy with duping the authorities. He travelled by train to Charleston, and in a fashion similar to Rubens', placed the *Commodore* under the suspicions of port officials. The beguiled officers at Charleston unwittingly followed the wishes of the conspirators to the letter and kept their revenue cutter in port in order to observe the known freebooter.[3]

Funston's own personal involvement with all these cryptic arrangements began at 7 P.M. on the August evening that he reached the Cortlandt Street Ferry in New York City. In company with other *expedicionarios*, he found himself under the charge of a *junta* agent who wasted no time with any social amenities. This closed-mouth revolutionary whisked his party of recruits across the Hudson River and through Jersey City to a track site

---

[3] *Ibid.*, pp. 232-233. On page 232, Footnote Number 8, Rickenbach relates how John "Dynamite" O'Brien, who was just one of many colorful characters whom Frederick Funston was to meet in his varied career, got his nickname. He allegedly safely transported by ship sixty tons of dynamite to a Colombian port by running through a rough ocean and a severe electrical storm. On pages 233-234, Rickenbach also relates that the *junta*, at the same time during which the *Dauntless* was sailing, hired the steamer *Laura* to take ammunition to Navassa Island, a landfall that was situated off the Southeastern coast of Cuba. While *en route* to its destination, the *Laura* met three American tugs off Jamaica and took on their cargo and men for Navassa. These sailing operations showed that Funston was indeed participating in one of the *junta's* large-scale, covert transfers of personnel and materiel from the United States to Cuba.

where a Pennsylvania Railroad sleeper was waiting. Before many minutes, the car started the group through the early August night toward Charleston, South Carolina, and Funston and his colleagues reached this destination without any difficulties.

Ensconced in a hotel in the sultry southern city, the *expedicionarios* from New York struck up some new acquaintanceships. They met with over thirty, upper-class Cubans, who were residents in the same hotel and who were also bound for service with the rebels. Funston noticed that also hanging about the hostelry were several groups of men who were trying their utmost to appear to be only ordinary guests. These loiterers were American private detectives. Some of them were in the pay of the Spanish ambassador, and others had been hired by federal agents. By striking up conversations, these sleuths earnestly strived to find out the schedules and destinations of the Cuba-bound party. A pair of them amateurishly tried to loosen the tongue of an amused Funston by offering to ply the Kansan's sweet tooth with an ice cream soda at a local confectionary. These espionage efforts all failed, partly because of their ineptness, and partly because the *expedicionarios* did not long remain exposed to the agents' clumsy blandishments.[4]

The expedition's stop-over at Charleston ended on the following day. Funston and the other recruits boarded one of the *Plant Line Railroad's* special private cars that was a coach on a regularly-scheduled train running to Jacksonville, Florida. A full night's travel in the exclusive vehicle, whose door guards barred all outsiders, brought the *expedicionarios* to Callahan, Florida. This hamlet was the junction point for two lines, the *Florida Central and Peninsular* and the *Plant Line*. It

[4] A. Prats-Lerma, "La Actuacion del Teniente Coronel Frederick Funston," *Boletin del Ejercito*, Nov.-Dec., 1931, p. 362; Frederick Funston, "To Cuba as a Filibuster," *Scribner's Magazine*, September, 1910, pp. 308-311.

was the location where the recruits' private car, the last on the string, left the Jacksonville-bound train and pulled out on a siding.

After a short wait, Funston noticed that his car joined a train that was being pulled by a *Florida Central and Peninsular* locomotive and then immediately retraced part of its journey. Next, at another siding, the car halted while the engine picked up three freight cars. Each of these cars bore heavy loads of Cuban-purchased arms and munitions that had originated in Bridgeport, Connecticut. At this point, the *junta's* plotters had completed making up their so-called "Fritot Special," and their new soldiers had successfully shaken off all pursuit. The expedition that was carrying Funston to Cuba was ready for the last stage of their land passage.[5]

In the wee hours of an August morning of 1896, the revolutionaries' abbreviated entourage puffed into the sparsely-populated rail crossing of Woodbine, Georgia. Carefully chosen by the *junta* because of its seclusion and easy access to the Atlantic Ocean, this tiny community sat by the side of the Saltilla River. Woodbine was, moreover, a safe sixty miles to the North of Jacksonville, Florida, where fully-deceived federal officers awaited in vain the arrival of the filibusters, who seemingly had vanished overnight.

At sunrise, the recruits began to unload the freight cars' war supplies, and Funston wryly noted that the cargo had been deceptively labeled "sawmill machinery" by the *junta*. They worked quickly under the hot Georgia sun to stow this valuable load aboard the *Dauntless*. Moored on the river bank near a bridge, the tug was about one hundred yards across sloping, sandy land from the tracks. Five hours' hard, sweaty work moved the entire contents of the cars. Funston recollected that the band of recruits altogether had transferred a twelve-pounder field piece, scores of artillery shells, numerous revolvers, rifles, saber-like machetes, saddles, and several hundred pounds of small arms ammunition from the wooden freight-vehicles to the tugboat.

By midday, the men were through with their chore, and they immediately climbed aboard the *Dauntless*. The laden tugboat was now under the command of John O'Brien, who had secretly made a rendezvous with the craft. The tug's whistle toots announced the beginning of the short passage down the Saltilla to the Atlantic, and Frederick Funston was on his way to his first tropical warfare.

In the meantime, some other precautions that the *junta's* scheme entailed had made it possible for the *Dauntless* to enjoy an unhindered passage away from the Georgia shoreline. In accordance with the operation's plan, the tugboat *Commodore* had already quashed an immediate danger of federal interference. Acting as a decoy, the *Commodore* had executed a coastwise voyage and steamed from Charleston, South Carolina, toward Hampton Roads, Virginia, on the evening before the *Dauntless* put out to sea. This cruise had successfully raised the suspicions of the captain of the district's coast guard cutter. Believing that he was hot on the wake of a gun-runner, this officer had turned his ship away from the mouth of the Saltilla River and sailed hard after the North-bound *Commodore*.

Though he was relieved that the *Commodore* had drawn off the Coast Guard vessel, Funston was soon confronted with a more mundane problem. Once the *Dauntless* reached deep water, he was seized by the enervating nausea of motion sickness. This was an ailment that always plagued him while he was water borne, and it lasted this time for almost the length of the trip to Cuba. Captain O'Brien, who wished to conserve coal for flank speed in case of pursuit, had inadvertently made this discomfort worse. He decreased the tug's speed drastically and thereby permitted the craft almost to wallow in the swells. So, instead of a swift, comfortable run to Cuba, the *Daunt-*

*less* chugged slowly through the waves and subjected her passengers to considerable tossing about.

As the craft neared the Northeastern coast of Cuba, Funston became aware of a threat that was far more perilous to him than a queasy stomach. In order to reach its beach rendezvous with *insurrecto* forces, the *Dauntless* had to pass close along the Cuban shoreline. Consequently, the danger of Spanish interception loomed large. General Rafael Cabrera, who was the military commander of the forty-three men of the expedition, and tugmaster Captain O'Brien decided to make defensive arrangements. They put the Kansas artillerist in charge of his four fellow, English-speaking *expedicionarios*. Then they delegated to Funston and his squad the task of rigging up the twelve-pounder on the bow of the tug as a deck gun. Funston made this emplacement quickly so that the *Dauntless* would have to run only in the event that she met one of the few, but powerful, Spanish gunboats that prowled the coastal waters. In case of an encounter with one of the numerous, lightly-armed patrol launches, the tug could fight off the enemy effectively with the breechloader. Funston's cannoneers secured the weapon with lines, shrouded it in canvas, and then they stood by, ready to fire at Funston's command, if the need arose.

No Spaniard appeared fortunately, and late in the afternoon of August 16, 1896, the sea trip's fourth day, the *Dauntless* neared its destination. The tugboat was not far from the port of *Neuvas Grandes*, and O'Brien made his turn for the shoreline at a point that lay off the land of *Camaguey* Province. Shortly after it had headed inland, the *Dauntless* put into an inlet that the Cubans called *"Las Neuvitas"* and dropped anchor. In spite of the fading daylight, the efficient O'Brien ordered landings to start at once. In a wink, cargo hatches came alive with grunting men, who commenced the off-loading of the heavy, but essential, war materiel. The goal of Funston and the others now was the beach, a

Funston and his men land their gun in Cuba.

sandy, surf-lashed strip that was about one-half mile from the anchorage site.[6]

When the men were ready to ferry their cargo to the shore, Cabrera put Funston, who was still chief of the English-speaking contingent, in charge of one of the eight flat-bottomed ship's boats. These small vessels were the means that the party intended to use to land the expedition. Of special concern to boat captain Funston was the specially-rigged bow gun that he had commanded late in the voyage. He piloted the piece to *terra firma* safely in his ship's boat, though he lost a few shells in the pounding surf. Others were not so lucky. Their boats capsized in the rough shallows and strew weapons and munitions along seven hundred yards of sandy beach. Luckily, no Spanish soldiers materialized at this critical juncture, and the only interruption to the ticklish work came after several hours' toil had transferred three quarters of the tug's load ashore. With frightening suddeness, the distant intrusion of a searchlight from a patrolling Spanish gunboat faintly illuminated the busy scene at *Las Nuevitas*. The ominous beam broke off all activity.

His steam kept up for just such an exigency, O'Brien at once put out to sea. By cruising in a large circle, he outdistanced the interloper and returned in a few hours to disgorge the final quarter of the cargo. In the meantime, Funston and his guncrew had set up their precious field piece behind a log that lay parallel to the beach at the edge of the forest. This position afforded both some cover and a good field of fire on the inlet. Positioned here, they could chastise any Spaniards who might land

---

[6] A. Prats-Lerma, "La Actuacion del Teniente Coronel Frederick Funston," *Boletin del Ejercito*, Nov.-Dec., 1931, pp. 361-362; Frederick Funston, *ibid.*, pp. 313-315; Rickenbach, *ibid.*; on page 362, Prats-Lerma listed the names of Funston's four English-speaking companions who accompanied him and thirty-nine Cubans on the voyage to Cuba aboard the *Dauntless*; they were: A. B. Peters, Charles Huntington, W. R. Wellsford, and Horace Walinski.

to investigate. Because nothing developed, the five soldiers-of-fortune turned to helping in the collecting of the scattered materiel and aided the other *expedicionarios* in landing most of the supplies successfully.

Afterwards Funston sought out his "considerable personal stuff," and found everything, including "a large camera," intact. Cabrera soon ordered the expedition to set up a hidden camp, and when they had done this task, the command settled down to await the arrival of the column of *insurrectos* whom they anticipated to come from the interior to meet them. In accordance with the *junta's* plan, the island *insurrectos* had earlier received word of the expedition's landing and had reputedly dispatched a force to accept the cargo and lead the novices to their new posts.

After nearly four days, 600 men, who were commanded by one of Maximo Gomez's subordinates, appeared. The column collected the newly arrived men and equipment and began the trek to the interior. At twilight on August 22, 1896, Funston discovered that he at last was in the heart of the insurgents' lands. He was, in fact, in the camp of the fierce and venerable Maximo Gomez. He was thirty miles from the beach landing site, and he was keen to get his first military assignment and taste actual combat. Frederick Funston was now an *insurrecto* deeply involved in the months-old Cuban struggle for independence.[7]

[7] Arthur Royal Joyce, Untitled and Uncited Article, October 29, 1917, F. Funston Papers, Box 75; Frederick Funston, *ibid.*, pp. 316-318; R. V. Rickenbach, "Filibustering with the *Dauntless*," The *Florida Historical Quarterly*, April, 1950, pp. 237-238. Actually, as Rickenbach pointed out, the *Dauntless* did not end her mission with the safe delivery of her cargo and recruits. O'Brien took the tug to a rendezvous with the *Laura*, and, in the absence of *The Three Friends* and the *Commodore*, the *Dauntless* took on more goods and carried them to points that lay to the West of Santiago on August 22 and August 24. In one week, the *Dauntless* landed contraband whose total value, including transportation, was $160,000. These deliveries embraced all sorts of materiel: two twelve-pounders with 500 shells, 2,600 rifles and carbines, 858,000 rounds of ammunition, as well as other equipment.

Funston and his guncrew set up their precious field piece behind a log.

# 4

## In the Context of the Revolution

The service that Frederick Funston rendered to the Cuban cause in the field lasted from August, 1896, until December, 1897, and came during the critical period of the *insurrectos'* struggle with Spain. Funston's experiences as a *guerrillero* in these seventeen months were shaped largely by the ebb and flow of the fortunes of war. What occurred as the Cubans fought the Spaniards over the entire island, both before and after his arrival, affected Funston's life considerably. Consequently, a broad survey of the important Cuban military events would place Funston and his adventures of 1896 and 1897 in the proper perspective.

Funston entered a conflict that was already months old. There was in progress a bitter, guerrilla-type war whose pattern had already been rigidly constructed by the combatants. A product of weeks of scheming by scores of dedicated Cuban *emigres* who had loitered in mainland cities between New Orleans and New York, the struggle actually began in extreme eastern Cuba on February 24, 1895. Although authoritarian Spain's colonial inefficiency and corruption were the ultimate causes of the uprising, the Cuban instigators availed themselves of an additional anti-Spanish current. They took advantage of the repercussions of the economic crash of 1893 in their island's economy to forward their program of national independence and make the break with the mother country.

At the outset, Maximo Gomez, the key rebel military leader, capitalized greatly on this economic adversity. He, together with other rebel leaders as well, recruited many *insurrectos* from the masses of his unemployed countrymen. Many other Cubans had seen their jobs vanish later with the exclusion of Cuban sugar from the United States by the Wilson-Gorman Tariff Act of 1894. A far-reaching protective measure that included provisions to aid economically distressed sugar producers in the United States at the expense of the Cubans, the 1894 measure hurt Cuban agriculture badly. Since the affected sugar growers and workers saw no prospects of re-employment, they were often willing to serve as soldiers for a cause that at least promised better times.

As the rebellion progressed, the *insurrectos* developed a plan for punishing Spain by further wrecking the island's agriculture system and using the distress to their advantage. Gomez, who was acting under the title of *jefe maximo*, was the first Cuban rebel to employ this devastating strategy. Shunning even the pretext of trying to win a decisive military victory over the Spanish army in the field, Gomez harshly applied the irregular terror of guerrilla warfare in order to free his country. On July 1, 1895, he issued general orders that set forth the tactics that his troops were to follow throughout the course of the conflict: Burn the sugar cane fields in order to destroy the life that the feeble island economy yet possessed; these crop fires were designed by Gomez to throw out of work even more farm laborers who would subsequently either join the rebels or flee to the congested cities; the *jefe's* secondary tactic was then to encircle these deprived, urban centers and ultimately reduce their displaced unemployed inhabitants to the state of starvation and thereby force Spain to capitulate. By these ruthless and desperate means, Gomez commenced to wage his war in mid-1895.

During these weeks, the old veteran's cause was

The fierce and renowned Maximo Gomez.

going well. Notable successes that his troops won in engagements against Spanish units in eastern Cuba, in fact, encouraged Gomez and the other rebels to make a significant move. They felt confident enough to proclaim a civilian government under President Salvador Cisneros Betancourt on September 19, 1895. While the new civil authorities governed "the liberated areas" that lay in the wilder, less developed eastern portions of the island, Gomez decided to take the war to the Spanish elsewhere on Cuba. He shifted the war aggressively into the wealthier, more populous western half of Cuba. Declaring in late September, 1895, that he would be near *Habana* by Christmas, the *jefe maximo* ordered the western planters not to grind their sugar cane that season. He warned that if they did go ahead and process their crop, they would find themselves treated as supporters of Spain by the *insurrectos*. More than ever, Gomez was determined to spread fire and desolation the length of Cuba and thereby force independence on the Spanish, who would, he believed, free Cuba because of the economic drain that holding the island placed on Spain's resources.

Gomez made good his promise. As 1895 drew to a close, the rebel bands were advancing steadily westward and leaving ravaged fields and destroyed buildings behind them along their line of march. By Christmas, Martinez Campos, Spain's aged Captain-General, was finished; his flying columns had been checked by the Cubans, and his garrisons were now impotent and unable to halt the rapidly moving guerrillas. On January 6, 1896, as fearful *Habaneros* gazed at a sky that had been made murky by the smoke of burning plantations, Campos cabled his resignation to Madrid. Fatefully, he also recommended that the government choose Don Valeriano Weyler y Nicolau as his successor. Unfortunately for the rebels, the home authorities accepted Campos' suggestion.

Weyler, who was a veteran soldier, knew Cuba well and had helped Spain contain the earlier Cuban attempt to gain independence, 1868-1878. Reputedly an energetic and ferocious fighter, Weyler was fresh from duty in the Philippines, where he had been instrumental in putting down a Filipino effort at throwing off Spain's colonial rule. He arrived in *Habana* on February 10, 1896. He came none too soon. Chaos was everywhere. The capital was almost completely isolated, since the rebels were holding all the major telegraph lines. Antonio Maceo, Gomez's able mulatto subordinate, was the main *insurrecto* leader on the scene. He had risen from private to general during the fighting in the earlier mid-century rebellion, and now he reigned supreme in the former wealthy region about *Habana*. Without question one of the best soldiers in Cuba's history, he was in complete charge of all territory that lay outside the Spanish-held, fortified cities of extreme western Cuba. Elsewhere in the western provinces, it was the *jefe maximo* himself who called the tune. Meanwhile, to the East, the provisional republic claimed full sovereignty over Cuba and considered the island an independent state.

The situation demanded strong measures, and Weyler began to apply them at once. On February 16, 1896, he issued stern proclamations that promised swift punishment to anyone who aided the rebels in the slightest way; he ordered virtually every Cuban to carry an identity pass; he instructed the islanders to evacuate certain country settlements; he authorized the trial of all suspects by courts martial. He also encouraged the sugar planters to bring in their crops and so tried to thwart Gomez's strategy of economic paralysis.

Such had been the general course of the Cuban insurrection prior to Funston's appearance on the strife torn island as a guerrilla fighter. The rebels had previously enjoyed considerable success, but by September,

1896, they were becoming aware that the Spanish, who were now under the command of the tough-minded Weyler, still possessed great perseverance. Funston's first weeks of service coincided with a renewed effort on the part of the Captain-General to regain the initiative that the Spanish had lost to the *insurrectos* while Campos was commanding the colony's defense.

Weyler reversed himself on his agricultural policy early in the fall of 1896. He decreed that he would not permit any grinding of sugar cane in the coming season. His purpose was to cut off Gomez's chief source of revenue, since the *jefe maximo* was levying a sort of tax on sugar producers who were naturally eager to protect their property from destruction and who thus would contribute to Gomez in order to save their estates. By this time, Weyler's forceful, police-state policy had somewhat stabilized conditions in western Cuba. The Spanish forces numbered close to 200,000, and the summer rains had slowed down guerrilla operations and provided the Spanish troops time to strengthen fortifications around the cities.

In addition, Weyler shored up defenses along the two *trochas*. These facilities were a pair of separate, fortified military railways that ran across western Cuba, from the South to the North. Weyler's tactics, together with the adverse effects of the wet weather, had combined to cut the insurgents' army into two large commands. There was the contingent that included Funston and operated in East-Central Cuba under the leadership of Gomez. There was another command of rebel elements that campaigned in the West. These Cubans were under the charge of Antonio Maceo, who was yet quite active.

It was Maceo's persistence that moved Weyler to inaugurate the use of the *reconcentrados* in western Cuba's *Pinar del Rio* Province on October 21, 1896. In adopting this ploy, the Spanish Captain-General only took a leaf from Gomez's book of tactics. He cleared the countryside of all people, livestock, and supplies in order to starve out the guerrillas. He ordered everyone to go into the fortified cities in order to deny to Maceo all potential recruits and labor. Later, much to the horror of American newspaper readers, Weyler extended the *reconcentrado* policy to other provinces.

As 1897 arrived, Funston, who by this time was already a battle-scarred veteran, knew that, in contrast to earlier months in the war, Spain's cause seemed on the rise. The able, dedicated Maceo was dead. He had been killed by bullets on December 7, 1896, in an accidental brush with Spanish soldiers. Maceo had broken out of his penned-up position that lay to the West of the *trochas*, and Spanish troops had blundered upon his camp and shot him without realizing his identity. With Gomez contained by strong Spanish units in central Cuba, Weyler began a thorough, broad advance whose direction ran from the West to the East. The determined Spaniard fought all rebels whom he found; he swept up all supplies that might in any way have been useful to the Spanish; and he destroyed anything of value that he left behind his columns.

By the middle of March, 1897, the insurrection was in deep trouble. Even Gomez himself was hard pressed by the enemy, and the rebels enjoyed freedom of movement only in the remote, wild eastern reaches of the island where Funston now was serving under the *jefe maximo's* subordinate, Calixto Garcia. Garcia could do little more than make aimless marches about the countryside. Only the threat of immediate starvation for his troops could force Garcia to launch an attack against even an isolated Spanish outpost. The hope of capturing victuals was the downcast Cubans' greatest goad to battle, and the prospects of independence for Cuba seemed bleak indeed.

Fortunately for the *insurrectos*, the summer rains of

1897 slowed the tempo of Weyler's effective campaigning. Bad though they were for the deprived rebels, these deluges were worse for the aggressive Weyler, who curtailed his troops' activities and gave the rebels respite. Hunted and hungry, Funston and his cohorts hung on desperately. As Funston completed his first year as *guerrillero*, a lucky break came. On August 8, 1897, an Italian anarchist, who was angered by the punishment that Spanish officials in Madrid had handed out to some of his Spanish colleagues, assassinated Antonio del Castillo Canovas, Spain's Conservative prime minister. As all Cubans knew, the extremist's victim was the key Spanish leader who had strongly backed Weyler's stern Cuban policy and assured the Captain-General a free hand on the island. After an interlude of "caretaker government," the Liberal Party's Praxedes Mateo Sagasta formed a coalition and assumed charge of Spanish government.

As a Liberal, Sagasta headed a group who had long been opposed to Weyler's methods and wished to reconcile the Cubans by an offer of broad autonomy within the framework of the Spanish empire. Accordingly, Weyler received a cable that ordered him to Spain in late September, 1897. For his replacement, Sagasta chose Ramon Blanco y Erenas, an officer who was willing to abandon his predecessor's strong approach. In mid-November, Blanco began to relax regulations in the *reconcentrados*, and on November 25, 1897, in the name of the crown, he issued a decree that granted Cuba an autonomous government. These fortuitous developments gave Gomez's and Garcia's followers a reprieve and revived their faith that ultimately they would triumph.

Spain's backing away from Weyler's forceful methods had a graver repercussion than that of revitalizing the hopes of the *insurrectos*. Weyler's approach, if it had been pursued rigorously by the Spanish army on Cuba, might have eventually ended the insurrection in favor of Spain. Blanco's policies only allowed the *insurrectos* to regroup and begin their guerrilla operations on a larger scale. Since the Spanish government was reluctant—or, unable—to see that milder tactics would not move the *insurrectos* to accept autonomy within the empire, but would only encourage them to protract the fighting, there was one possibility that became more and more a certainty as 1897 ended: Intervention by the United States in the Cuban insurrection.

Such intervention materialized as "the Spanish-American War" in the spring of 1898. This short conflict not only had import for the Cubans' cause but also far-reaching implications for the United States. It marked the arrival of the North American republic upon the world scene as an imperial power. And, interestingly in view of the part that he was to have in helping acquire this new empire for his nation, Funston was deeply involved in this long-drawn-out island rebellion in Cuba.[1]

---

[1] David F. Healy, *The United States in Cuba, 1898-1902: Generals, Politicians, and the Search for Policy*, pp. 4-5, 8-9, and 36; Frederick Funston, "A Defeat and A Victory," *Scribner's Magazine*, December, 1910, pp. 754-755; Henry Houghton Beck, *Cuba's Fight for Freedom and the War with Spain*, pp. 223-230, 233-234, 238-247, 252, 257-258, 267, 270, 273-276, and 288; Howard Wayne Morgan, *William McKinley and His America*, pp. 327-328; Richard Harding Davis, *Cuba in War Time*, pp. 17-19 and 26-27; Walter Millis, *The Martial Spirit*, pp. 1-2, 10-11, 16, 23, 31-32, 34-35, 40-42, 46, 53, 55, 59-61, 66-67, 74-76, 79-81, and 87-88; both Beck and Davis were strongly biased against the Spanish and openly championed the *insurrectos* and called for intervention by the United States; however, Beck disclosed many of the proclamations and orders of the revolution, in full and in English; he also described several of the prominent personalities who were involved in Cuban affairs, 1895-1898; Davis, who was an experienced war correspondent, gave good brief, eyewitness descriptions of Spanish fortifications, both around the cities and along the *trochas*; see *Cuba in War Time*, pp. 13-14, 77, 91-94, and 100; two

more recent books that provide both colorful details and provocative interpretations of United States and Cuban relationships in these epical years at the turn of the century are: Philip S. Foner's *The Spanish-Cuban-American War and the Birth of American Imperialism,* Volume I, 1895-1898, and Volume II, 1898-1902, (in paperbacks), and John A. S. Grenville's and George Berkeley Young's *Politics, Strategy, and American Diplomacy: Studies in Foreign Policy, 1873-1917.*

Though marked by a strong Marxist bias, Foner's two volumes rest in part on Cuban sources with which most North Americans are unfamiliar, and Foner presents interesting and enlightening accounts of some aspects of the Cuban side of the story; his work can be useful in offsetting some of the ethnocentric outlook, either conscious or unconscious, that has characterized many treatments of the events of 1898 that have originated in the United States.

Grenville and Young approach the problem of "the Spanish War" from an altogether different angle, that of the national executive and legislative branches of government in Washington, D. C.; they deal with the motives, aims, and pressures at the top levels of government where diplomacy took its final shape.

Together, Foner's and Grenville's and Young's books afford a fairly broad and balanced look at the problem of the Cuban Insurrection, 1895-1898, Cuban-United States relations, and the war of 1898 and its repercussions; see Foner, Volume I, pp. 1-118; Volume II, pp. 406-421, 559-577; and see Grenville and Young, pp. 179-296.

# 5

## The First Test of Battle

However welcomed they were by the Cuban *insurrectos*—Ramon Blanco's policies were of little consequence in late 1897 to Funston personally. The Kansas *expedicionario* was too debilitated and sick to take any serious concern in the revolution's outcome. Funston felt that his very survival depended upon his leaving Cuba at once and getting immediately back to the United States, where he could have adequate rest and medical care. His protracted rigors had been many, and he believed that he had indeed done his part to free Cuba.

Funston's train of rugged military adventures began shortly after the Cabrera expedition, guided by their formidable escort, had marched toward the interior. The first phase of the trek brought the sizeable column to a small settlement whose name was *"Los Angeles de Salvial."* This was a place that the *insurrecto* officers believed to be secure enough to allow them to use it as a point for a distribution of the newly-arrived arms and ammunition. Funston performed his first island duty as an artillery expert by climbing atop a conveniently located mound of earth and directing the cleaning and oiling of the new cannon. For several days, the men of Cabrera's party busied themselves with refitting and supply activities. Then, on August 29, 1896, Funston got his first peek at a renown revolutionary leader when *Generalissimo* Maximo Gomez, the *jefe maximo*, marched in with his troops to take a share of the new materiel.

After Gomez had been in camp several hours, a group of Cuban officers led Funston and his fellow *expedicionarios* before the famed chieftain. This old fighter appeared, so Funston thought, just as the published photographs of the times portrayed him—lean, wiry, and swarthy, his face appointed with a thin, white moustache and goatee. Reputedly a stern and high-tempered man and a native of Santo Domingo, the revolutionary leader had passed the morning by going over the mail from the *junta* that had been brought in by the *Dauntless*. He wished personally to greet the North American recruits, all of whom held the famous guerrilla leader in awe.

Gomez first thanked Funston for his volunteering. Then he bluntly inquired about the extent of the Kansan's artillery knowledge. When he had admitted his limited expertise, Funston learned that he would have the grade and privileges of a captain, a rank that Gomez ordered the Cubans to date from August 16, the day of the expedition's arrival in Cuba. However, Gomez also gave Funston to understand that his was a captaincy that would be without the usual powers of command until he had actually proved himself as an artillerist.

A subsequent query of the *jefe maximo* turned the *expedicionario's* attention to sugar cane, the staple of the rebels and omnipresent crop of the island. Smiling grimly, Gomez used his Moorish blade to demonstrate to Funston how to strip the cane and get to the nourishing pulp. Then the *insurrectos'* leader amused himself by watching the recruit try inexpertly to get at the sweet plant with his own newly-issued machete. This incident firmly fixed Funston in the mind of Gomez, who afterwards always addressed him as "*Capi*." This abbreviated form of the rank "*Capitano*" was a term of endearment. Also, Gomez jokingly often asked Funston upon encountering him in camp how he liked being a *"Mambi,"* a pejorative Spanish term for an *insurrecto*.[1]

In these first few days with the rebels, Funston also made acquaintance with the pattern of life that he would be leading for the next sixteen months. To his surprise, he found that almost all his fellow soldiers who were serving with him under Gomez were white men. They came mainly from either *Puerto Principe* Province or *Camaguey* Province rather than from the heavily Negro populated provinces of *Santiago de Cuba* and *Manzanillo*. The officers, whose pay was always in arrears, were in civilian life mainly landowners and professional men, many of whom, having studied at universities in the United States, possessed a fair knowledge of English. Well-mounted and wearing the Cuban tricolor on their straw hats, these commissioned fighters were impressive, even though they wore only the plain white cotton ducking of the Cuban countryside. For weapons, they carried revolvers and the two-and-a-half foot long cavalry machetes that had been manufactured by a firm headquartered in Providence, Rhode Island.

In the ranks were the men who before the war had

[1] A. Prats-Lerma, "La Actuacion del Teniente Coronel Frederick Funston," *Boletin del Ejercito*, Nov.-Dec., 1931, pp. 361-363; "Cuban and Philippine Island Documents," F. Funston Papers, Box 76; Frederick Funston, "Cascorra, The First Cuban Siege," *Scribner's Magazine*, October, 1910, pp. 385-386; Frederick Funston, "To Cuba as a Filibuster," *Scribner's Magazine*, September, 1910, p. 318; while Funston remembered the insulting Spanish word for an *insurrecto* as "Mambi," Foner, Volume I, pp. 31-32, relates that the Cubans who fought as insurrectionary guerrillas were known to the Cuban people collectively as "Mambises," a plural version of Funston's "Mambi"; according to Foner, the term—like the *jefe maximo* himself, Maximo Gomez—originated on the neighboring island of Santo Domingo, where one Juan Ethninius Mamby, a black man and a Spanish officer, defected to the Dominicans during their successful fight for independence from Spain in the 1840's; Spanish soldiers referred to the troops of Mamby as "Mambises," and later, in 1868 and afterwards, many of these same Spaniards, who came to Cuba to suppress the insurrection there, applied the term "Mambises" to the Cuban rebels, who themselves picked up the appellation.

been small farmers, mechanics, store clerks, town laborers, and employees of the big landowners. Usually unpaid like their officers, these enlisted men looked like tropical tramps. They wore ragged, white ducking uniforms, straw hats, and they often went barefoot. Rusty and ill-maintained Spanish Mausers, bolt-action, clip-fed rifles captured from the enemy, provided weapons for about a quarter of the rebels. The remainder used equally ill-kept, American-made Remingtons. These weapons were breech-loaders, and Funston believed that they were good rifles.

These Cuban foot soldiers also carried the shorter machete that they used in many ways: In close fighting, in chopping cane, and in constructing camps and fortifications. The discerning eyes of artillerist Funston observed that their bandoliers always seemed well filled by new cartridges. Funston concluded at once that these troops were not bandits lacking in military procedure and regulation. While they had acquired only enough drill to enable them to deploy themselves in battle formations readily, the *insurrectos* operated under well known rules and followed the "strictest discipline."

Early in the morning of August 24, 1896, Funston's schedule initiated him into additional aspects of his new life as a *guerrillero*. The whole force arose at 3 A.M., marched toward the interior at first light, and made a camp in the rolling uplands about 11 o'clock. On this day, the volunteer artillerist, whose improving colloquial Spanish allowed him to avoid any serious language difficulties, learned a routine that was to vary but little in the coming weeks. Following the early reveille came "breakfast"—if the men had any food and were not on the move. This meal was always accompanied by a hot liquid that was in the form of a coffee-like, sweetened water. The Cubans called this eye-opening beverage *"sambumbia."* An hour later there was a roll call. This was a practice that the *insurrectos* repeated at 5 P.M. whenever they were languishing in camp and not actually campaigning across the countryside. In camp, the bugle was the rebels' major instrument of communication, and it sounded retreat precisely at 8 P.M. Then the notes of the call for silence and sleep rang out at 9 P.M. At this time, everyone of the *insurrectos* removed all his clothing and bedded down in the canvas sling that he carried. The troops hung these hammocks between two trees in order to avoid having the numerous island insects for their bedmates.

Funston by necessity learned the ways of these swaying sleeping devices, because, shortly after coming shore, he lost his "large rubber blanket" that he had intended to use as his basic bedding. The impermeable piece was a veteran of Funston's previous jaunts into the wilderness. It had disappeared from its perch on the saddle of Arthur R. Joyce, who had come to Cuba four months earlier. Joyce was with the *insurrectos* who came to meet Cabrera's group.

The loss of the rubber item angered Funston, who subsequently found himself bereft of most of his considerable hoard of personal baggage during his first days on the march. The Kansan and Huntington, another *Dauntless expedicionario*, in spite of Joyce's friendly warning, erred grievously and let friendly Cubans help them carry their heavy loads of private gear. Predictably, all their things vanished in the mysterious, unaccountable ways in which such articles often do in armies. Even the camera that Funston had purchased in order that he might be able to illustrate the articles for *Harper's Weekly* was appropriated by unknown hands. Before long the artillerist was left with little of his original kit, except a Spanish grammar book and the clothes he was wearing. These were garments that had been trail-worn by Funston in Death Valley and Alaska. They were Funston's trade-mark among the *insurrectos* for weeks, since he continued to prefer them over the prevailing white duck. They consisted of a "ragged hunting coat and [a pair of] badly soiled corduroy trousers," and they were unique garb for someone who was engaging in tropical warfare.

Though he was piqued at the mysterious rebels who had made off with his belongings—he used "vigorous [and] explosive" language to register his feelings publicly—Funston bore no grudges. Before many days had passed, he was manifesting a strong friendship toward his Cuban comrades, and he was freely entering into off-duty, social activities, such as they were. He learned that entertainment appeared in the guise of such simple amusements as chatting, playing cards, singing, and reading and re-reading the weeks-old newspapers that had come in surreptitiously from the United States.

Funston also observed that the daily fare of his comrades and himself was as uncomplicated as the diversion. In time of plenty, the staple of the rebels' diet, aside from the ever-present sugar cane, was a meat and vegetable concoction. It was a kind of stew that the Cubans called "*aijacco.*" This dish was a field ration that the encamped soldiers gathered in groups of four or five to cook over cedar fires. Little knots of mess mates devoured this stew twice daily, at about noon and near 6 P.M.

Later during his stay in Cuba, the famished Funston ardently longed for *aijacco*. After things had turned worse for the rebel forces, he subsisted for weeks entirely on yucca, sweet potatoes, and pumpkins. The rebels broiled these plants over coals and ate them devoid of any spices, because they had none. Aside from the pressure of Weyler, this dearth of food stemmed from the fact that the *insurrectos* rapidly consumed all the beef that was available in the areas where they carried on protracted campaigning.

To offset these food shortages, the rebels sometimes were compelled to break up their tactical units. On these occasions they divided their commands into groups of from fifty to five hundred men and scattered them far and wide over the countryside so that the *guerrilleros* might set up new camps and seek supplies in a fresh region. These smaller units scoured the terrain for miles for cattle to provide fresh stew and jerky and break the tedium of a purely vegetable diet.

Funston also found out that scarcity was the rule in the Cubans' medical department. In this part of the *insurrectos'* army, medicines were at times in short supply, and physicians were few. In consequence, nearly all of the *insurrectos* who had served any length of time suffered either from some form of ailment or from poorly healed wounds that proper care might have cured. The omnipresent affliction was fever, since the troops' primitive, outdoor living and continual campaigning exposed everyone time and again to tropical diseases of various types. Later Funston accumulated first-hand knowledge of the Cubans' difficulties in looking after their sick and lame. These were the shortages and inadequacies that came close to killing him.[2]

In early September, 1896, Funston learned from Gomez of his assignment in the pending attack on *Cascorra*, a fortified town occupied by a tough unit of *Catalonians*. Though Funston informed the *jefe maximo* that his gun lacked the necessary shrapnel shells, the Cuban leader continued nevertheless to plan his assault, since he intended to use the siege of the Spanish outpost as a ploy to draw out a relief column of regulars. Gomez hoped to encounter the succoring formation on favor-

[2] Anonymous Newspaper Article, Uncited, Marked, "From a Kansas Paper of January 11, 1898," F. Funston Papers, Box 75; Anonymous Newspaper Interview with E. H. Funston and Charles F. Scott at Iola, Kansas, F. Funston Papers, Box 75; Arthur Royal Joyce, Untitled and Uncited Article, October 29, 1917, F. Funston Papers, Box 75; Emory W. Fenn, "Ten Months with the Cuban Insurgents," *Century*, June, 1898, pp. 304-305; Frederick Funston, "Cascorra, The First Cuban Siege," *ibid.*, pp. 386-387; Frederick Funston to E. H. Funston, March 5, 1897, In Camp, Headquarters, Department of *Oriente*, Cuba, F. Funston Papers, Box 75; Frederick Funston to Frank Webster, April 10, 1897, In Camp, Headquarters, near *Holguin*, Department of *Oriente*, Cuba (Uncited Newspaper Reprint), F. Funston Papers, Box 75; Webster was a friend of Funston and lived in Lawrence, Kansas.

able terrain and destroy it in open-field combat. After testing the twelve-pounder at a site in the countryside and finding the piece in good working order, Funston prepared to support Gomez's attack. Following his orders, he went ahead with General Javier Vega, a staff officer, to make a foot reconnaissance of *Cascorra's* defensive perimeter and select an advantageous spot for the artillery emplacement. Funston noted that the 170-man Spanish garrison, who had been aided by some sympathetic Cuban volunteers, had constructed a formidable position.

The hard-working regulars had turned the church, the city hall, and a tavern, all thick-walled edifices, into interlocking strongpoints. Each of the village's stout structures had become a redoubt that the Spanish had well-loopholed, heavily-sandbagged, and interconnected with the others by deep trenches protected by barbed-wire. Funston longed for the presence of a heavy siege gun. He realized that his aiming instruments permitted him to carry out only direct-line-of-sight firing, and that accordingly the gun and crew would be exposed to direct counterfire by the Spanish riflemen. Still, he gave in to the wishes of General Vega and decided to take a chance. He agreed to set up his twelve-pounder in a level grassy field at a place that lay only a scant 400 yards from one of the enemy's strongpoints.

Funston, who fully realized that he was going against orthodox artillery principles, kept his objections to himself. He swiftly readied himself and his six English-speaking artillery subalterns for their first combat together. That night, he witnessed for the first time the Cubans' preparations for the emplacement of his field piece. The islanders employed techniques on this occasion that they were to use over and over again before cannoneer Funston left the Cuban interior. First, the infantrymen, who were temporarily acting as sappers, drove two parallel rows of wooden stakes into the ground. These lines of posts were two feet apart and showed about six feet of timber above ground. Between these stakes, the perspiring soldiers tamped down earth, and they held the packed soil in place by means of lateral pieces of wood that they affixed near the base of the line of stakes and fence rails that they attached along the top. In the middle of the construction that was called a *"trinchera"* by its builders, there was a door-sized space, whose purpose was to serve as a gun port.

Though this structure gave the ammunition and some of the crewmen protection, Funston, who sighted the piece, and the four other *expedicionarios*, who acted as loaders, received little cover from the arrangement. Aware of this inadequacy, but determined to take part in the attack, Funston tried vainly to catch some sleep. At 4 A.M., he placed himself behind the Hotchkiss twelve-pounder and was joined by four of his English-speaking soldiers-of-fortune. Near at hand was the 100-man Cuban infantry support, who were nervously awaiting the battle's commencement. Gomez's only other gun was a two-pounder that was manned by the two remaining artillerymen. This piece stood ready to fire at the enemy town from another site.

At dawn on September 22, 1896, Funston announced the opening of the siege by firing a round that scored a hit on the second story of the fortified stone tavern. Since he had found the range immediately, he soon pounded this structure to rubble. Then he shifted his sightings to the heavily built-up church and the municipal building, and his accurate gunnery soon forced the defenders to take refuge in the outlying trenches. When tall grass partially obscured his aim, and when the Spanish trenches proved invulnerable to his flat-trajectory fire, Funston decided that an alternation of tactics was in order. During a lull, he went to headquarters and sought the permission of Gomez to move his gun after dark to a position that was even closer to the Spanish entrenchments.

The Cuban leader consented, and Funston returned to his field piece. He used the remainder of the day to throw a very slow, harassing fire into *Cascorra*. That first night in camp as he oiled and cleaned his cannon and prepared it for its new emplacement, Funston once more talked to the venerable rebel commander. Gomez did not seem insulted by the novice *expedicionario's* presenting a new plan that called for a bold attack. Funston's idea was to make a direct assault and seize the stronghold he believed was the key to *Cascorra's* defenses. This objective was an earthen redoubt that contained about one-half the Spanish garrison. Funston proposed that Gomez send an infantry force against the position as soon as the twelve-pounder and the two-pounder had reduced the covering fire of the church bastion to ineffectiveness by means of a concentrated bombardment. Gomez, however, rejected the plan, since he feared to order his relatively inexperienced men to undertake an assault directly against barbed-wire entanglements that were covered by concentrated Mauser rifle fire. He did not want to risk a defeat that might demoralize his command, which was unused to regular siege warfare. He was conserving his strength in order to meet the Spanish relief force in the open field and win a clear victory on his own terms.

Funston passed the second day of the siege by trying to reduce the church bastion by a slow fire. Such a bombardment meant that he was releasing his shells at the rate of one round each half hour. Not surprisingly, he felt strong impatience at the indecisiveness of this contest, especially since it was his first taste of battle. His fellow cannoneers' Anglo-Saxon frustration equalled his own. There was also the ammunition factor. The small hoard of shells for the twelve-pounder was rapidly running out, and even the remainder of the missiles was not altogether dependable. Many of the warheads had been striking their targets without detonating. This matter of dud rounds was a problem that was to plague

Funston and his artillerymen serve their field gun during the attack on *Cascorra*.

artilleryman Funston incessantly during his Cuban service. Time and again, either because of dampness or
because of improper handling in transit, shells proved
defective in combat and thereby considerably lessened
the effectiveness of Funston's guns.

The shell problem, this time combined with the
artillery contingent's persisting impatience, gave rise to
another plan for a decisive infantry attack on *Cascorra*.
After conferring with his half-dozen gunners, Funston,
who was accompanied by subaltern Walter N. Jones of
New York City, again called on the *Generalissimo* at his
headquarters. On this visit, Funston requested that the
*jefe maximo* permit him to do two things. Gomez
should allow him to subject the church bastion to a
furious hour's bombardment. Then immediately after
the shelling, Gomez should let another *expedicionario*
and himself lead a force of 200 picked Cuban infantrymen in an assault on the battered target. Funston now
maintained that the works by the church were the
critical element in the town's defenses.

Funston argued that if the Spanish should attack the
assaulting party from the earthen redoubt, Gomez could
send in another force against them. Though Funston's
warm enthusiasm almost won acceptance of the plan,
Gomez's caution ultimately held sway. Consequently,
the final decision was one that Funston did not really
like. But, Funston held his peace. He felt that because
he had asked for a change, he could not refuse one, in
spite of its unsatisfactory form. Gomez ordered his men
to build yet another *trinchera* for the Hotchkiss twelve-
pounder. This emplacement was to go up at a site that
was within only 200 yards of the tavern stronghold and
that was thus within easy range of numerous Spanish
rifles.

The result of the general's decision was that a hot
fire-fight enveloped Funston and his artillerymen on the
third day of the siege. From their loopholes, the defenders of the tavern could easily see the filibustering can-

noneers as they served their smoking weapon. Time after time, Funston blasted gaps in the parapet of entrenchments about the fort. And, time after time, the trenches' defenders, who were covered by the fire of riflemen who were inside the bastion, quickly replaced the torn-up sandbags.

The Spaniards' marksmen aimed careful shots at Funston personally. Whenever the Kansan revealed himself for the two seconds that were necessary for him to sight the piece, he drew scores of slugs his way. One Mauser bullet careened off one of the cannon's trunnions almost at Funston's nose and sent him reflexively scrambling for cover. Predictably, the fire on the vulnerable position before long became too intense to allow servicing the gun. Funston and his cannoneers had to abandon their weapon and take refuge in a ravine, though they returned during a lull and dragged the gun to a safe location in the rear.

For the fourth day of the siege, Gomez again repositioned the twelve-pounder. He ordered his artillerymen to place their bigger gun near the crest of a low ridge at a site that was about 1,500 yards from the church fort. This place was well away from the dangerous rifle fire, and Funston thought that his weapon was well set up at this location. The barrel of the weapon now lay in line with both the church strongpoint and the earthen redoubt that sat at a point that was 300 yards on the far side of the church. Already learning to be economical with his ammunition, Funston intended that his over-shots of the church position should fall on the more distant stronghold and so not go to waste. Though they sustained only a slow fire throughout the day, Funston's artillerists almost completely exhausted their ammunition before sundown. Thereafter, until October 5, 1896, the last day of the investment, the cannon remained almost altogether silent, and the cannon tenders had very little fighting to do.

Finally, the indecisive action reached a climax.

Gomez heard from his scouts that a Spanish relief column at last was approaching, and he consequently decided to break off the combat and move out to meet the interlopers. He ordered the cannoneers to move their gun to a position that was within only 180 yards of the tavern. When they had sighted their piece, they were rapidly to expend all their remaining ammunition in a last barrage and do as much damage as possible. Subsequently, they were to join in the general withdrawal of the Cubans from the town's perimeter.

Funston and his crew carried out these orders faithfully, and they were involved in a heavy exchange with the enemy throughout the last day of the siege of *Cascorra*. Under the cover of darkness and in the midst of a heavy rain, the *expedicionarios*, who were now technically veterans, joined the Cuban evacuation. Their artillery was useless until more shells arrived, and they relinquished their two guns to a special body of Cubans, whom Gomez had commanded to move them to safety.

With this last inferno of shelling, Funston had passed through his first test of battle. Later he remembered this episode at *Cascorra* as something that had definitely been characterized by "an awful roar" and as much smoke as a Kansas prairie fire. One of the six artillerymen who was serving under him had caught a bullet in the thigh on the eighth day. Funston had experienced his own close calls. A bullet grazed along the bottom of his left foot and split his shoe from toe to heel. Like his men, he was physically jaded after the battle, and, given the outcome of the siege, he was somewhat disappointed. Now, because of an ammunition shortage, he was temporarily freed from his duties as an artillery chief. There was much fighting ahead, and Funston, together with his crew, was about to act for the *insurrecto* cause in another guise.[3]

[3] A. Prats-Lerma, "La Actuacion del Teniente Coronel Frederick Funston," *Boletin del Ejercito*, Nov.-Dec., 1931, pp. 363-364; Frederick Funston, "Cascorra, The First Cuban Siege," *ibid.*, pp. 388-401; Frederick Funston to Frank Webster, April 10, 1897, *ibid.*

# 6

## In the Thick of It

The new role for artillerist Funston and his band of gunners was that of cavalrymen. Armed with carbines, they participated in three days of hard, mobile combat with their 900 comrades against the 2,500-man Spanish relief column under the command of General Jimenez Castellanos. Following his quick abandonment of the siege of *Cascorra*, Gomez deployed his force to intercept the Spaniards at a meadow three miles to the West of the battered town. Known as "*La Mancha*," and located forty-seven miles to the East of the city of *Puerto Principe*, this field was the place where, at 4 P.M. on October 6, the Cubans initiated an hour's engagement. This was Funston's first cavalry action, and it ended in failure, since Castellanos brushed aside Gomez and pushed on to *Cascorra* to succor the beleaguered garrison.

However, the *jefe maximo* had only begun to harry the Spanish force. Within a few hours, Funston and his gunners again fought as mounted soldiers. At 3 A.M. on October 7, 1896, an excited scout brought some news to Gomez, who was now encamped not far from *La Mancha*. The report was that the relief column was trying to evade a second encounter with the Cubans by making a stealthy early-morning evacuation of the rubble-strewn *Cascorra*. Again Gomez showed his willingness to fight, and he decided to catch the Spanish in the open and hit them while they were on the march and not tactically deployed to repel an attack.

The grizzled general ordered the command to move out at once. In a drizzling rain and heavy darkness, the Cuban column trudged amidst much confusion one-half mile to the North. In a short time, Gomez put his men into a position that lay astride the *Camino Real,* the suspected Spanish route of march. Once in place, they remained motionless until daybreak when Funston heard the reports of distant, scattered shots. Within minutes, he saw scouts ride in to inform Gomez what had occured. The Spanish, who were still trying to avoid the rebels, had forsaken the highway and cut to the North in an attempt to reach the railroad and relative safety at a junction whose name was "*Las Minas.*"

Gomez once more aggressively went after the enemy. All day long, Funston's column moved rapidly along a line of march that was two miles from the Spaniards' route, yet parallel to it. Though he heard intermittently the dim rattle of remote rifle fire, Funston did not believe that a large battle was about to develop immediately. He correctly surmised that Gomez, who was definitely not interested in mere harassment, had decided to head off the Spaniards and meet them in open combat after all.

Only when the scouts brought word that the Spanish had finally stopped for the night at a spot on the main road that was about two and a half miles from the village of *San Miguel de Nuevitas* did Gomez allow his own weary men to halt and rest. There was no food for Funston and his fellow *insurrectos*, because the day's rapid march had not afforded the Cubans time to kill cattle and cook rations. Low whistles pried the Cuban troops out of their hammocks after only fitful slumber. Still clinging to his battle plan, Gomez was straining again to get astride the Spanish line of march, deploy his men in combat formations, and gain a victory in the field. This time, only an hour's jostling through the inky night put the command where the *jefe maximo* desired it to be. It was then that a ravenous and bone-tired Funston dismounted, sat down with his back propped against a tree, and wearily waited for daylight.

At 4 A.M. on October 8, the general's order to mount put the worn artillerist in the saddle for the second cavalry encounter of his life. The Cuban commander had mustered almost 500 mounted men for this scrape that the rebels later named *"Desmayo"* in honor of a near-by estate. Keenly aware of the time factor, Gomez speedily made his last dispositions. First, he ordered the medical detachment to set up a hospital in the woods and designated one hundred dismounted men to protect the installation. Next, he divided his 479 horsemen into two ranks and placed them both across the road at a spot that was situated about a mile away from the bivouac. Finally, the general himself took up a post with his staff on the extreme left of the line. Funston, who was with the other *expedicionarios,* found himself on the extreme right flank of the formation.

Gomez's battle plan was a model of simplicity. He intended to surprise the head of the Spanish column as it came up the road in march order and throw the entire enemy formation into confusion. He believed that he could break up the Spaniards' ranks with the shock of the charge of his horsemen, who would subsequently pursue the fleeing infantrymen and do terrible execution among them with their carbines, revolvers, and machetes.

Two unforeseen factors, however, modified this scheme and placed Funston and the other cavalrymen in a precarious situation. At first light, a heavy fog settled down about the Cuban formation and limited visibility to ten yards. Funston noticed that all the men were close to terror as they nervously waited for the leading ranks of the enemy column to emerge from the impenetrable mists.

The other factor was the battle wisdom of the Spanish commander. His island experience had led him to anticipate the Cuban deployment and order his men to alter their formation accordingly. To Funston and his fellow *expedicionarios* on the right wing, the scene created by these Spanish movements was quite eerie. They heard the distant jingle and rumble made by over 2,000 of the enemy who were seemingly advancing toward their position. As these sounds got louder and louder Funston and his group strained their eyes to peer through the damp haze; then suddenly everything became quiet to their front.

At this point, a slight breeze began to ease the excruciating tension by slowly blowing aside the fog and permitting Funston to make out the mounted Cubans who were to his left in a formation that stretched 300 yards across the road and beyond. The sun rose as the wind wafted across the field. Within half an hour, the artillerist discerned to the front at about 400 yards what at first he thought was either a fence or a hedge. As the light improved, he and the other *insurrectos* realized that the object was a wedge-shaped, massed Spanish infantry formation, whose front ranks were kneeling while the rear ranks were standing. The rifle of each *soldado* sported a fixed bayonet, and the Spanish commander had drawn up the entire assemblage across the road. The Spaniards' angle pointed directly at the horsemen, and, behind it, the enemy had deployed two field pieces. Without doubt, the Spanish troops were ready to receive a cavalry attack, and Gomez was compelled by the changed situation to revise his plan. He had either to attack the prepared infantry or to withdraw quickly and let the enemy proceed.

For a few moments, Funston and his companions discussed in hushed, nervous tones the possibilities open to the *jefe maximo*. The rebel bugle sounded the charge and ended all speculations. The entire double line surged forward. First advancing at a trot, then rushing at a gallop, the Cubans shouted and brandished their carbines defiantly. Before the two ranks of horsemen had advanced more than forty yards, they met the artillery cannister and rifle fire of the Spanish, and the din of battle increased. Funston estimated that each enemy Mauser expended a half-dozen full magazines during the brief interval in which the Cubans tried to close with their serried opponents.

During this nearly quarter-mile run to the Spaniards' position, Funston was in the middle of a classic, early-nineteenth-century, cavalry movement of the time of Napoleon I. Gomez's charge was a tactic that pitted the dash and shock of horsemen against the fire power of massed infantry, who were supported closely by artillery. Fortunately for Funston, neither the magnitude of the encounter nor the accuracy of the musketry was Napoleonic, because the majority of the 2,000 Spanish soldiers fired their rifles much too high to inflict a mass slaughter on the rebels. Nonetheless, carnage there was, and it was damaging enough to send screaming horses and cursing men crashing to the ground right and left around Funston as he charged the Spanish.

When, after a few mad moments, they reached the Spanish ranks, Funston and his comrades proved as un-Napoleonic as the enemy's riflemen. They failed to throw their mounts into the Spaniards' bayonets and smash the infantry line. Rather, they halted along a line that was from twenty to forty yards in advance of the foot soldiers, who were all the while frantically firing their bolt-action weapons. Funston and the Cubans rode up and down the Spanish front and discharged their pistols and carbines into the enemy's ranks with good effect. Funston saw that the Spanish, fearing that the *insurrectos* might break their infantry, quickly withdrew their two cannon to safety. Yet the Spaniards did not panic and abandon their defensive, wedge-shaped formation. After a minute or so of the perilous confrontation at close range with these stubborn ranks of Spanish troops, Funston and his cohorts knew their position was indeed precarious; either the Spanish had to collapse and flee, or the Cubans had to withdraw and suffer heavily under a volley of rifle fire as they broke off their attack.

At this critical juncture, a sudden fusillade struck the Spanish ranks from the extreme right of the *insurrectos'* line of attack. A reserve force of 300 Cuban infantry had come into action. Firing American-made Remingtons, whose big, white, puffy clouds of discharged powder always cloaked the battlefield in smoke, these rebel foot soldiers soon enfiladed one arm of the Spanish "V." Within minutes their shooting did what the cavalry had not done and forced the enemy to fall back. Since the enemy preserved good order, however, the mounted Cubans, who had already taken considerable losses, did not immediately press the Spanish during their retirement. The brief, furious cavalry charge at *Desmayo* was over.

Funston had participated in a five-minute action that saw the Spanish infantrymen and cannoneers either kill or wound over half the 479 Cuban horsemen. Many horses were either slaughtered or injured by the Spaniards' shots, and only 100 men of the original assault force remained mounted at the battle's end. Months later, Funston learned that the Spanish had also suffered considerably in the scrape at *Desmayo*, where they sustained 204 casualties, counting both the killed and the wounded.

The Spanish soldiers had employed their fast-firing, Mauser rifles and their pair of breech-loading artillery pieces against the *elan* and the side arms of the Cuban cavalry. When he reflected on the event in later years, Funston concluded that the affair at *Desmayo* was a notable event. He believed that the feat that the mounted rebels had performed in the Cuban savannah on October 8, 1896, was more heroic than that carried out by the famous British Light Brigade at *Balaklava* in the Crimea almost a half century earlier. He was probably overly sanguine in this estimation. At any rate, the bloody episode varied his growing repertoire of combat experience.

Funston had little time to reflect on the event at *Desmayo* while the smoke still hung over the battlefield. Maximo Gomez, doggedly seeking a victory, organized a pursuit of the retreating Spanish column. Later in the day of October 8, in fact, Gomez so closely harried the enemy that General Castellanos took a special precaution. The Spanish commander set up his artillery in the town of *San Miguel de Nuevitas* and assigned his gunners the task of beating back the Cuban advance. In the Cuban attack upon *San Miguel*, Funston had his horse, the first of seventeen mounts that he was to lose one way or another in Cuba, shot from under him by the Spanish, though he himself came out of the fighting unscathed.

Artilleryman Funston subsequently distinguished himself to the *jefe maximo* when one of the Spanish artillery rounds fell into the midst of the Cuban command post without exploding. Funston rushed to the scene, dug up the warhead, unscrewed the fuse, and presented the harmless missile to Gomez as a souvenir of the day's events. There was no doubt afterwards that Funston was known and appreciated by the Cubans and their leaders.[1]

General Maximo Gomez's plans gave Funston an-

[1] A. Prats-Lerma, "La Actuacion del Teniente Coronel Frederick Funston," *Boletin Del Ejercito,* Nov.-Dec., 1931, pp. 363-364; Frederick Funston to Charles F. Scott, November 9, 1896, In Camp, *Puerto Principe* Province, Cuba, F. Funston Papers, Box 75; Frederick Funston, "Desmayo—The Cuban Balaklava," *Harper's Weekly,* March 5, 1898, pp. 225-226.

other opportunity to strengthen his reputation by displaying his martial bent in another way. Following the clashes around *Desmayo*, the *jefe maximo* marched his 1,000-man command to another area in order to meet the contingent of Calixto Garcia. The rendezvous was at a point a few miles to the East of *Cascorra*, and it was not far distant from the town of *Guaimaro*, a Spanish stronghold that sat in extreme eastern *Camaguey* Province.

When they had made contact, the two Cuban leaders held a formal military conference without delay. They decided to invest *Guaimaro* with their combined forces, whose strength at this juncture numbered nearly 3,000 men. While no doubt the two chieftains drew confidence from this sizeable force, Gomez and Garcia also took heart from the initial performance of Funston's artillery unit. In fact, Gomez had specifically complimented Funston and his cannoneers in a general order that he issued shortly after the abortive siege of *Cascorra*.

Funston naturally took pride in Gomez's special recognition of his efforts, but he was further elated now because of the caliber of the *insurrectos* whom he encountered at the rendezvous. The high character and dedication of the renowned rebel Calixto Garcia, his staff, his officers, and his men in general profoundly impressed the Kansan. He soon learned that this 2,000-man establishment possessed its own artillery and, as well, its own band of *expedicionarios*. There were two field pieces. These guns were supervised by five North American officers, and a sixth volunteer from the United States, who was a North American physician, helped in the running of the medical department.

The leader of this clique of mainland *guerrilleros* was W. D. Osgood, a former college football player. Osgood was a man with whom Funston quickly became a fast friend. Indeed, all the volunteers seemed companionable and eager for company of their countrymen. It did not take Funston long to discover that his English-speaking associates and he were in complete accord on many things. There was one thing on which everyone most ardently agreed: General Garcia was a most unusual and admirable man.

To Funston, this revelation was most satisfying, since he had already concluded that the hoary guerrilla fighter was a most impressive figure. With his heavy-frame and over six feet of height, Garcia, whose snow-white shock of hair and great white moustache denoted wisdom and experience, seemed to be the ideal field commander to Funston. Moreover, there was something additional that Funston believed added a touch of invincibility to the *jefe's* romantic reputation. Funston could not help but notice a fact that at first took the beholder's attention away from the massive, wizened features of the old warrior. There was a round hole stuffed with cotton in the center of Garcia's forehead.

This grisly aperture served as a dramatic reminder to everyone of Garcia's experience in "the Ten Years' War." When the Cubans had made an unsuccessful bid for independence over a quarter of a century earlier, Garcia had joined the rebel cause and fought for it hard. At one point the then young *insurrecto* was hard pressed by the Spanish, and, fearing his capture and subsequent execution, he made an attempt at suicide by shooting himself in the head with his pistol. However, the Spaniards did not let him die. Rather, they rushed him to a military hospital, where the skill of a Spanish surgeon saved his life. The enemy also spared him execution, and a generation later, he was still fighting the Spaniards for Cuba's independence.

Funston and the other *expedicionarios* believed that this veteran *insurrecto* was a most approachable man

Calixto Garcia

and was both dignified and kindly. The Kansan noted that while they held Gomez in awe, the volunteers held Garcia in deep affection. Funston felt especially attached to Garcia because of the cordiality and courtesy he had received at his first meeting with the famous rebel figure. On October 13, 1896, at the plantation known as "*San Antonio de Blanquizal,*" Garcia, who spoke good English, extended a personal thanks to Funston for his service thus far to the Cuban cause. He also praised Funston for his obvious enthusiasm for action. Then, because of his esteem, Garcia arranged to assign Funston to his own command. Such recognition and courtesy placed Garcia well up on Funston's list of favorite people.

Also ranking high in the estimation of Funston was Colonel Carlos Garcia. The son of Calixto Garcia, Colonel Garcia remained one of the Kansas artilleryman's friends for years. Still another Cuban whom Funston especially admired was Mario Menocal, who was a staff officer and graduate of Cornell University. Funston discovered that these two English-speaking officers acted as informal *ombudsmen* to the volunteers, and that they were always willing to consider the North Americans' special problems and complaints.

The people who collectively comprised "a most interesting study" for Funston, however, were the Negroes of General Garcia's command. Recruited by the *jefe* mainly in *Santiago* Province, these *insurrectos,* in Funston's opinion, were far more aggressive than their counterparts who lived in the northern cities of the United States. As an officer in the Cuban artillery, Captain Funston rated a "striker," or personal servant, about whom there was something quite noteworthy. A trans-Atlantic shipper had brought this man to Cuba from western Africa in the illicit slave trade of the 1870's. Funston observed that his striker conversed with

some of his fellow blacks from time to time in a dialect
that he concluded was a Congolese tongue.[2]

In spite of this heterogeneous racial composition,
Funston, who could never entirely shake his turn-of-the-
century mainland racism, thought that the men of the
two combined commands were potentially good soldiers. He saw that they were determined to take *Guaimaro*, even though the place lacked civilians to liberate.
He concluded that this fort town held great emotional
value for the Cubans, since it had been the seat of the
rebel body that had drawn up a constitution and designed a national flag in 1869 during the "Ten Years'
War."

Garcia and Menocal took Funston with them and
reconnoitered the prized town on October 15, 1896. At
first sight, Funston as an artillerist, noted that
*Guaimaro's* fortifications were strong and numerous,
including eleven strongpoints, or *"fortines."* The 300-
man garrison had surrounded all but one of these centers with barbed-wire entanglements that protected
"standing trenches." These were rifle pits that were
constructed partly above ground by the Spanish. They
were deep enough to allow a man to stand and fire and
yet remain under almost complete cover. Funston decided that the key to the entire bastion was *"Fortin
Gonfu,"* a blockhouse sitting on a low hill to the North
of the town. He reasoned that his artillery could domi-
nate the Spaniards' strongpoints from this post once the
Cuban infantry had seized it. He soon had occasion to
test his theory and verify his ability as an artillery
tactician.

On the night of October 16, 1896, Gomez, who was
the senior of the two insurrectionary generals, set up his

---

[2] A. Prats-Lerma, *ibid.*, p. 364; "Frederick Funston," *Harper's Weekly*,
March 5, 1898, p. 226; Frederick Funston, "The Fall of Guaimaro,"
*Scribner's Magazine*, November, 1910, pp. 579-580.

combined headquarters at a site about one mile to the North of *Gonfu*. He prepared to attack at once. Nearby were Funston and the *expedicionarios*, with the command's four pieces of artillery: two twelve-pounders and two two-pounders. Gomez designated a twelve-pounder to demolish *Gonfu*, the fortress considered impregnable by the Spaniards, and he put Major Osgood in charge of the gun. Gomez ordered Osgood to emplace his gun in a trench just 500 meters from the fort. The *jefe maximo* decided to hold the other twelve-pounder in reserve, and he put this second big gun under the command of Funston. He temporarily gave the Kansan the duty of an artillery observer and told him that his particular task was to aid Osgood's crew in finding the correct ranges to their targets.

The siege began at 7 A.M. on October 17, 1896. Funston watched Osgood's bombardment long enough to note that it was largely ineffective because of the stoutly-built nature of the Spanish trenches and because of the large amount of defective ammunition that failed to detonate. Then, Funston joined Osgood and his men behind the Hotchkiss field piece, whose heavy powder charges were creating tremendous recoils. However, he stayed in the artillery trench only a few minutes.

A 60-man force of the *insurrecto* infantry that was commanded by Menocal determined to make a "do-or-die" attack on *Gonfu*. Characteristically chafed by inactivity when action was at hand, Funston attached himself to this enterprise. He linked up with three other heretofore unoccupied artillerists and joined in the foot assault that dislodged the Spaniards. Subsequently, Funston passed the remainder of the day in the conquered *Gonfu*. Now, he was spotting targets for Osgood's cannon, whose crew had ensconced their piece in the seized blockhouse. His only injury occurred when he rushed precipitously to the aid of a wounded colleague. Clambering down *Gonfu's* observation ladder, he slipped and

Funston and his crew fire their field gun from a captured block-house at *Guaimaro*.

fell several feet to land on top of Osgood. The blow knocked both *expedicionarios* out of their senses for several minutes, though neither suffered any ill effects for long.

On the second day of the siege, however, the fighting did bring serious injury to Osgood and deep grief to Funston and his fellow *expedicionarios*. The twelve-pounder was hotly firing at innumerable targets from inside *Gonfu*, and the lethal piece became an intolerable torment for the Spaniards, just as Funston had anticipated. The harassed defenders of *Guaimaro* detailed a sharpshooter to fire on their lost post and silence its gun. Funston quickly became aware of the Spanish sniper's attention. He was in and out of the blockhouse, drawing fire as he moved and called off ranges to Osgood, who was sighting the cannon.

Funston had a close call while he was engaged in this range-finding. A round whistled through a loophole that was adjacent to the position in the rear of the gun where he was standing. The former footballer, however, was not so fortunate as his Kansas mate. As he leaned forward to make a windage correction, Osgood took a bullet through the forehead. Rendered senseless, he lingered for four hours without ever regaining consciousness. When Osgood died, Funston and the other *expedicionarios* experienced for the first time the immense shock of losing one of their own tight, little band.

Funston felt that there was an almost noble aspect to Osgood's demise. His admiration of the manly qualities that Rudyard Kipling, his favorite author, believed war brought out in soldiers peeped through his sorrow. He concluded that a quick battle death in behalf of a worthy cause was far and away a better mode to depart this life than was a lingering, bedridden dying that was brought about in stages by an emaciating disease. Funston was profoundly moved by the words Maximo Gomez said over Osgood's uncoffined corpse. The Cubans laid the *expedicionario* to rest in a grave marked only by a *mango* tree. Funston thought that such a ceremony was true; it was honest, and it did not smack of the maudlin sentimentality that characterized the usual funeral service. Funston concluded that a soldier's death was an honorable and fitting way for a real man to die.

Funston's views on death were incidental to the struggle at hand, and the siege dragged on. Within a few hours of Osgood's death, Gomez overruled Garcia, who surprisingly favored another North American, and appointed Funston to be Osgood's successor. Funston's new post bore the title "Artillery Chief of the *Departmento del Oriente*." The job meant that Funston took charge of all the artillery operations of the siege, and he was soon aware of the weight of his increased responsibilities. His duties now ranged from making tactical decisions to solving supply problems.

On October 20, 1896, the fourth day of the siege, a damaged powder charge caused a misfire in *Gonfu's* twelve-pounder. With a live round lodged in its barrel, the weapon was useless. After some difficulty, Funston procured a Cuban mechanic who spent several hours of delicate, dangerous work restoring the piece. As head artillery officer, Funston had to make some crucial determinations. He had to decide when to reduce and later, when to cease altogether, artillery fire as his four guns depleted their meager ammunition reserves.

As the siege progressed, Funston began to think of himself as an experienced veteran. He took close note of the military lessons that he saw about him. For the first time, he recognized certain shortcomings of the *insurrecto* forces. He saw that the Cubans' lack of a regular commissary department created unnecessary hunger. He was certain that the *insurrectos'* failure to abide by even the rudiments of proper field sanitation engendered avoidable pestilence. As a participant in the insurrection, he was indeed learning important practical lessons about soldiering in combat.

Gomez was preparing plans for a night attack on October 27, 1896, that would give the Kansan an additional instruction—victory. Since he had received a supply of artillery shells by pack train, the *jefe maximo* envisioned a large role in the effort for Funston's guns. He ordered Funston to lay down a general shelling of the Spanish positions throughout the day preceding the attack. To make this bombardment more effective, Gomez commanded Funston to emplace his pair of twelve-pounders in a trench that was only 400 meters from two of the Spaniards' remaining key *fortines*. The *generalissimo* moved his headquarters to the same trench.

At 6:30 P.M., one of Funston's pieces fired a signal round, and the assault commenced. The Cuban infantry rapidly pressed into the town without the usual fanfare of bugles and shouting. Within a few minutes, the Spanish strongpoints capitulated, and Funston, who was quite pleased that he had definitely "had a pretty finger in the pie," left his guns to watch the ebullient Cubans celebrate their *coup* and loot the enemy's stores. One last Spanish bastion, a strongly-fortified infantry barracks, held out until morning and afforded Funston another chance to show his martial skills. Aided by Cuban infantry, he worked one of the light-weight, two-pounder Hotchkiss guns by hand through the streets to within a few feet of the Spaniards' loopholes. Then, exaggerating somewhat, Funston announced to the enemy he was ready to blast their stubborn post to oblivion with his two-pound projectiles. Shortly the Spanish filed out in surrender, and all of *Guaimaro* was Cuban again.

Funston esteemed the victory as "a regular 4th of a July of a time." He thought that the triumph was a real tonic for the morale of the *insurrectos*. He heartily approved of the way that the Cubans humanely and willingly returned their wounded Spanish prisoners to their own government in order that they could get proper medical care.

Funston received a personal jolt from this benign policy of the Cubans. While he was present as an observer at the exchange site in a neutral meadow, he was greatly embarrassed by a fellow rebel's tactless remark. Reveling in the joy of victory, a Cuban soldier pridefully pointed Funston out to a severely wounded Spaniard as the artilleryman who had been the inflictor of his suffering. Disconcerted by this incident, Funston did not have time to fret over it for long. For the following week, he was involved with the revitalized Cubans in a bitter, peripatetic fight that successfully turned back a Spanish column trying to retake *Guaimaro*.

Funston's part in all these events that took place about *Guaimaro* was significant and widely known, as the episode with the injured Spaniard at the prisoner exchange showed. The Cubans intended to reward such outstanding service, and on November 12, 1896, Funston rose to the *insurrecto* rank of Major of Artillery. At the same time, he officially became the chief of all the artillery operations in the eastern half of Cuba. Both Generals Gomez and Garcia approved of his new commission, and they dated it from October 28, 1896, the time of the official fall of *Guaimaro*, because they maintained that he had indeed proved his merit as an artillerist during that operation.

Aside from this rise in his military status, Funston accrued other advantages from the Cuban victory at *Guaimaro*. By rummaging around in the stores of the enemy's captured commissariat, the new major and one of his men procured enough rations to allow the artillerymen of the eastern theater to eat relatively well for two whole months. In addition, Garcia's largess provided his gunners with a sum of $100.00 to divide among themselves. Funston also came into a private stipend at this happy juncture, since the revolutionary government awarded him personally another $100.00 in recognition of his duty well done. Now, with Gomez departed toward the West for *Santa Clara* Province, Funston was commander of four guns, and he was ready to follow the future orders of Calixto Garcia in the East.[3]

[3] Arthur Royal Joyce, Untitled and Uncited Article, October 29, 1917, F. Funston Papers, Box 75; A. Prats-Lerma, *ibid.*, pp. 364-365; "Cuban and Philippine Island Documents," F. Funston Papers, Box 76; Frederick Funston, *ibid.*, pp. 580-595; Frederick Funston to Charles F. Scott, November 9, 1896, In Camp, *Puerto Principe* Province, Cuba, and Frederick Funston to Charles F. Scott, May 10, 1897, In Camp, Headquarters, Department of *Oriente, Mejia*, Cuba, F. Funston Papers, Box 75.

# 7

## Campaigning With Garcia

For the next five months, November, 1896, to March, 1897, Funston served with Calixto Gracia in a manner that was often strange for a cannoneer. He acted more in the capacity of a roving guerrilla than he did as an artillery officer. During these weeks, the *insurrectos* who were under the control of Garcia moved virtually at will through eastern Cuba's *Oriente* and *Camaguey* provinces and engaged the Spanish in a variety of actions. Accordingly, Major Funston took part in ambushes of supply convoys; he participated in hit-and-run assaults on Spanish posts; and he played a role in numerous, small-scale siege attacks that Garcia's men carried out against isolated Spanish garrisons.

Funston also helped to run down the pro-Spanish, native-Cuban *guerrilleros* by acting as a cavalryman in encounters in which both sides always displayed great savagery and brutality. The loyalist Cubans, who were actually royalist guerrillas, usually operated as fast-moving bands of cavalry, and they were especially hated by the Cuban *insurrectos*. These Spanish auxiliaries made a practice of hunting out the rebels' secluded hospitals and mercilessly slaughtering everyone whom they found in the wards. Funston learned that in return the outraged and vengeful *insurrectos* gave their turn-coat countrymen no quarter whatsoever. The rebels always remorselessly killed any of the pro-Spanish *guer-rilleros* who fell into their hands.[1]

Although they were somewhat unsettling to all of the artillerymen, these practices between *insurrectos* and *guerrilleros* did not mar service with the Cuban cause for Funston. The ten weeks of late 1896-early 1897 that followed the siege of *Guaimaro* were the high point of satisfaction for Funston as an *expedicionario*. He was a veteran. He was still in good health, and he was unwounded. He was well liked by the Cuban leaders, who had recognized his merit with promotion, praise, and pecuniary reward. Proud of his record, Funston believed that his elevation to colonel was only a matter of time. Moreover, he "certainly enjoy[ed] the respon-sibility and power of . . . [his] position" and took grati-fication from his signs of status, having his own cook for his mess and his own groom for his horse.

Funston found the every day life of a soldier in the field most attractive during this period. The rains were over. There was yet ample fresh beef to devour in accompaniment with a generous amount of "liberated" Spanish rations. Sweet potatoes remained still a novelty to his palate, and he was thriving on the edible, banana-like *platana* and other "bric-a-brack [that were] peculiar to the tropics." His basic wants cared for and new adventures unfolding daily, Funston was quite con-tented.

There were several important additional explana-tions for Funston's "halcyon days" of service with the

---

[1] A. Prats-Lerma, "La Actuacion del Teniente Coronel Frederick Funston," *Boletin del Ejercito*, Nov.-Dec., 1931, p. 365; Frederick Funston, "A Defeat and a Victory," *Scribner's Magazine*, December, 1910, p. 735; one should not confuse the terms *"guerrilleros"* and *"insurrectos;"* the Cuban rebels always thought of themselves as *"insurrectos,"* though in the broad historical sense, they often used traditional tactics of guerrilla fighters; they always pejoratively spoke of the Cuban loyalists as *"guerrilleros,"* a word that bore evil connotations.

Cuban cause. There was an abundant presence of something that Funston had sorely missed and come to crave during his lengthy second Alaskan trip of 1893 and 1894. This element was the camraderie of a coterie of likeable and admirable friends. Funston and his eight artillerists of Garcia's command constituted a tightly-knit group of companions. They were bound closely together by common experiences and common interests. All of them liked soldiering, and five of the six who survived the island war later served in the United States Army. Thrown together constantly by the rigors and demands of war, the men enjoyed a prolonged association that did not dilute any bonds of friendship; rather, it strengthened them.

During their slack times, the group enhanced the ties that battle had created. They swapped stories, and Funston often offered entertainment to his artillerymen by telling them of his adventures as a newspaperman in Fort Smith, Arkansas, and as a botanist-explorer in Death Valley and Alaska. Sometimes the cannoneers joshed their Kansas major into giving them his recitations of bits of Kipling's verses, since they knew that he dearly loved these fragments of poetry. Sometimes they sang together. When he had his choice of which selection to do, Funston would render in his monotone bellow either the church hymn "Beulah Land," his favorite piece, or "Marching Through Georgia," the Civil War song that he always offered with great gusto. Though he was a far better *insurrecto* soldier than he was a songwriter, Funston even composed a unit song for his command, who, on occasion, would raucously sing Funston's lyrics to the tune of "On the Bowery."

While all this easy companionship made campaigning somewhat pleasureable in these winter days, there was something else that made the war less of a burden for Funston. He maintained his faith that the Cubans' effort was a noble crusade and that the Cubans were a fine people. He thought that in the future he was going to be proud that he had helped the Cubans eject the Spaniards from the island. He was also optimistic about the course of the war. Funston believed that in the coming spring the fighting would be done and Cuba would be completely free and independent.

Dangerous military adventures still appealed to Funston in late 1896 and in the first days of 1897. He simply liked his work, because it meshed well with his ideas of adventure. These were concepts that Funston had in large measure gleaned from the romantic versions of soldier episodes that he avidly read in his earlier years. He declared that it was "a great thing to have read Kipling, before one mix . . . [ed] up in some real fighting and . . . [saw] the bullets 'kicking up the dust spots on the green' as they . . . did in the ballad, *Gunga Din*, . . ."

Funston still intended to write his own accounts of his military experiences in this Cuban service. By mid-November, 1896, he had written two articles and dispatched them to *Harper's Weekly* in New York City. Though they apparently never reached their destination, this pair of battle stories revealed that Funston still thought of his life as exciting, adventurous, and worthy of relating in writing for others to read. So, Funston continued to think of a possible future as a writer and reporter at this time. Yet, uppermost in his mind, there remained the sentiment that he was leading the best of all possible lives. Funston believed that many others would eventually envy him and admire his achievements.[2]

Given such enthusiasm and earnestness, it was some-

[2] Arthur Royal Joyce, Untitled and Uncited Article, October 29, 1917, F. Funston Papers, Box 75; Frederick Funston to Charles F. Scott, November 9, 1896, In Camp, *Puerto Principe* Province, Cuba, F. Funston Papers, Box 75.

what ironic that Funston drastically altered his outlook
on the Cuban insurrection during the days of late January and February, 1897. As the new year progressed,
the war became more and more a burden and a grinding
bore to the Kansan, and his men as well. Militarily,
Garcia and his command were finally feeling the pressure of Weyler's relentless offensive by February, and
this turn of events did a lot to discourage the Kansas
*expedicionario*. Funston was suddenly learning what
war was like when a strong enemy held the initiative and
operated offensively. The command moved constantly,
because it was necessary to do so in order both to evade
the Spanish and to scrabble for a bare subsistence.
Funston and his gunners were compelled by this adverse
turn of events to bury their guns for a time. They had
very little ammunition, and since the artillery horses
were too weak to pull the pieces because of the lack of
proper feeding, Funston concluded that only a secret
cache could save the invaluable weapons from enemy
capture.

Nevertheless, Funston still thought of himself as a
soldier. He considered himself to be relatively a lucky
man in spite of these military reverses. Officially, he was
yet the artillery chief in the East, directly the commander of a pair of four-gun artillery batteries, whose
weapons were "steel breech loading rifles of the very
latest pattern . . ." He believed that his North American
officers were "good fighters." He confidently thought
that the men under him, provided the ammunition,
could yet "make things mighty hot" for the Spaniards.

Funston also tended to believe that he led a
charmed life. By his own reckoning, he had already
come safely through two siege operations, eight large-
scale battles, and "several" smaller struggles. Though two
of his horses had fallen in combat to Spanish bullets
while he was riding them, he had not in the least been
injured by the mishaps. One of these animals had col-

lapsed and died within a few feet of a Spanish position. Funston, who was mindful that the Spaniards were usually poor marksmen and that bridles and saddles were very scarce items, had decided to bring out his paraphernalia. After temporarily withdrawing from the scene, he had crept back to the enemy's line, moved up to the carcass of his mount, retrieved his cavalry equipment, and returned to his comrades, untouched by Spanish bullets.

Yet, in spite of his soldierly bravado, the Cuban war had lost its aura of romantic adventure for Funston, as March, 1897, arrived. For one thing, Funston by this time had abandoned his project of writing a series of articles about his experiences for *Harper's Weekly*. It was well nigh impossible for Funston to get his material out of Cuba and safely to the states. It was also true that the novelty and excitement of soldiering with the *insurrectos* had worn off. Island campaigning no longer stimulated Funston's imagination. Rather, when he projected his vision of the future, Funston now thought only of a practical business venture in railroading on the island republic once the fighting had ended and independence materialized. He looked upon his friendship with Major General Garcia as a decided asset, since he believed that the beloved rebel leader would certainly be the Cubans' first president. He admitted that he harbored "some big schemes in regard to railroad franchises in . . . [his] head" and that accordingly he was "glad to stand in with him [Garcia]."[3]

[3] Anonymous Newspaper Interview with Frederick Funston, Topeka, Kansas, *Daily Capital*, January 12, 1898, F. Funston Papers, Box 75; Frederick Funston to E. H. Funston, March 5, 1897, In Camp, Headquarters, Department of *Oriente*, Cuba, F. Funston Papers, Box 75; Frederick Funston to Frank Webster, April 10, 1897, In Camp, Headquarters, near *Holguin*, Department of *Oriente*, Cuba (Uncited Newspaper Reprint), F. Funston Papers, Box 75; Thomas White Steeps, "Funston Starving—Report That The Young Americans in The Insurgent Army Are Starving," Uncited Newspaper Article, May 5, 1897, F. Funston Papers, Box 75; Steeps was "a

Such a pecuniary, mundane interest was another indication of Funston's growing disinterest in soldiering. The railroad scheme was reminiscent of the coffee enterprise of 1894-1895, a project that, coming after his surfeit of adventures in the wilds of Alaska, had registered his disenchantment with further Arctic exploration. One factor that brought about Funston's growing discontent with *insurrecto* service stemmed from the unrelenting hardship and deprivation that Garcia's forces were experiencing during the late winter and spring of 1897. For days at a stretch, Funston and his *insurrecto* comrades were so lacking in sufficient food that they were at times actually "delirious from hunger." Often, their only ration for an entire day "consisted of a few sticks of sugar cane which . . . [they] chewed [,] swallowing the juice, . . . ." At night, during these involuntary fasting periods, Funston frequently awoke "from a troubled sleep in which . . . [his] dreams had been of bacon and kindred things."

By late April, 1897, Funston, who had been sorely missing pie and pastry as early as November, was avidly craving wheat products. He had not "tasted bread or anything that contain . . . [ed] flour" since he departed the mainland the previous August. Though dried meat was occasionally available, roots, herbs, and some tropical fruits were now Garcia's troops' dietary mainstays. Of this class of vegetarian edibles, the sweet potato, or

special correspondent of the Scripps-McRae League of newspapers" who visited Cuba, made contact with Garcia's *insurrectos*, and talked with Funston and his artillerymen during the early spring of 1897; he left Cuba by way of Jamaica from whence he dispatched his "scoop" by cablegram to the United States; he capped his sensational feature with the claim "that the Americans attached to the army of the insurgents [had] asked him to appeal to the State Department to do something for their relief;" probably, what lay behind this declaration was the feeling that was prevalent among Funston and his fellow *expedicionarios* that the United States should intervene in the Cuban revolution and halt the protracted suffering on the island.

tropical yam, appeared most often at meal times. Funston usually ate his yam as he crouched over a small campfire. Always he used a banana leaf for a plate and a stick for a fork, since there were no eating utensils available. Often, when he vented his hungry frustration, Funston would exclaim, "The same food—always the same food—yams—how I hate yams!"[4]

Making the inadequacy of rations even harder to bear for Funston and his comrades was the absence of proper shelter and clothing. These essential items were always in short supply with Garcia, though they were prerequisites for an army's good health, even in the mild climate of tropical Cuba. Funston had no tent (there was not even one for General Garcia) and slept under a shelter in the field only five nights during his entire service in Cuba. As he put it in later years, "We simply ignored the weather." He possessed no blanket, either for himself or for his horse. His underwear had long been non-existent by the spring of 1897, and he went five months without any interior garments at all. He had already discarded his worn-out hunting coat and dirty corduroy trousers. For days now, his military costume had been the usual rebel outfit of white cotton duck, panama hat, and sandals; of course, he wore this footwear without socks, the garments that he most missed. His whole kit "consisted of a hammock, a pancho, [a] revolver, [a] machete, [a] pair of field glasses, the clothes on . . . [his] person and not one other thing."

Funston's appearance reflected the rigors of this

[4] Frederick Funston to Charles F. Scott, November 9, 1896, In Camp, *Puerto Principe* Province, Cuba, F. Funston Papers, Box 75; Frederick Funston to Frank Webster, April 10, 1897, *ibid*,; Frederick Funston to Major General Leonard Wood, December 1, 1913, Headquarters, Hawaiian Department, Honolulu, H. T., Leonard Wood Papers, General Correspondence, 1913, Box 73, Mss. Division, The Library of Congress, Washington, D.C.; Thomas White Steeps, "Funston Starving—Report That The Young Americans in The Insurgent Army Are Starving," *ibid*.

protracted period of hardship and suffering. He was as shaggy, unkempt, and tramplike a figure as any other *insurrecto*, either officer or trooper. His beard and moustache were heavy and untrimmed; his hair was long and uncombed, and it poked out through the many holes that were evident in his beaten-up panama hat; his loose cotton shirt was streaked with dirt and faded; his ducking trousers were shreaded into strips that dangled below his knees and prominently revealed grimy, sandled feet. There was a bizarre yellowish cast to his skin, a feature that Funston called "that brown powdery effect." This tint was the result of Funston's bathing in the muddy waters of the *Cuato* River and then having to dry off in the sun without the benefit of any towels.[5]

Any observer who was familiar with the perils of living in the tropical wilds and who could have seen Funston during these weeks might have mistaken this yellowish cast for a tell-tale sign of something else—the dreaded "Yellow Jack," or "Yellow Fever," the scourge of the Caribbean. Fortunately, Funston did not contract this fatal malady. He did become afflicted with malaria during the first part of 1897. Called *"paludismo"* by the Cubans, this disease took a severe form in Funston's body. It caused him several times a week to burn with fever, fall into a delirious state, and finally undergo a "depressing chill in which it seemed that . . . [he] was trying to shake his teeth out." This affliction remained with him for many years after his Cuban stint, and, from time to time, it forced him to forego his duties and go on the sick list.[6]

---

[5] "Frederick Funston," *Harper's Weekly*, March 5, 1898, p. 226; Frederick Funston to Major General Leonard Wood, December 1, 1913, *ibid.*; Thomas White Steeps, "Funston Starving—Report That The Young Americans in The Insurgent Army Are Starving," *ibid.*
[6] F. F. Eckdall, "'Fighting' Fred Funston," Speech in *The Kansas Historical Quarterly*, Spring, 1956, p. 81; Frederick Funston, "A Defeat And A

Distressing as they were to Funston and his men
during these days of 1897, the malaria and the physical
privations alone could not have appreciably mitigated
the *expedicionarios'* ardour for the Cuban cause. Psychological factors, too, played an important part. They
probably were more instrumental in changing the attitude of Funston and his *expedicionario* band toward the
war than were the more obvious sufferings. The foreign
volunteers felt alone and completely cut off from their
families and friends. This feeling of separation resulted
largely from the inability of the *insurrectos'* supply
organization to bring in personal mail regularly from the
United States. Funston himself considered that getting
"no mail . . . [was the] worst hardship" that he encountered during these bleak weeks, and always he was
on the *qui vive* for more of the precious missives from
home.

Adding to this sense of estrangement was the view
that began to prevail among Funston and his artillerymen by the end of March, 1897. The English-speaking
group concluded that the war was endless. They now
abandoned all of the preceding days' romantic enthusiasm that had moved them to predict a Cuban victory
and peace by springtime of 1897. Reflecting this pessi-
mistic opinion, Funston conceded that, Spain, "that
grim old mother of nations," was "a plucky dame," and
she would be able to drag on the fight indefinitely.
Although he believed that Cuba would finally achieve
independence at some future day, Funston dismally
concluded that unless the *insurrectos'* side won out
"before a year, the island . . . [would] be all but
ruined." He harbored somewhat embittered views about
his own country's role in this relentless conflict. In his

Victory," *Scribner's Magazine*, December, 1910, pp. 750-751; *Medical
Report Form*, Manila, Luzon, Philippine Islands, September-November,
1901, A.G.O. 142866, Documents File Index, "Funston, Letters Received," *N.A.R.S.*, Washington, D.C.

eyes, the United States was "playing a damnable dirty part" in the rebellion. He was irked because, while he thought that his government "would flare up like an old hen" if a European power intervened, he also recognized that it was doing nothing while, a scant few miles away, "there . . . [was] being carried on, one of the most merciless and cruel wars in the history of mankind." The brutality of the insurrection, in truth, was yet another element that served to enhance Funston's war weariness and eliminate the romance that at one time had surrounded the island conflict.

The consequence of all these mental pressures was that Funston began to think of getting out of the Cuban war during the spring days of 1897. In May, he revealed to his sister that he intended to return home by the next October "and let them fight it out among themselves." He decided that he had been "a pretty big fool to come down . . . [to Cuba] and mix up in this War, . . . ," and he would undertake no such ventures ever again. He also reflected his disenchantment and low morale of this time in a letter that he directed to newspaperman Charles F. Scott, his close friend at Iola. He was, so he reported, staying through the fall campaign, only because General Garcia, whom he immensely admired, had "pressed . . . [him] so strongly" to remain and command the essential guns in the pending battles. He wrote that it had pained him to learn from Scott's earlier letter that most of his "old chums" were married, since "a man . . . [was, and rightfully so,] never so thoroughly a chum after he . . . [was] married as [he had been] before . . ."

Then, with his reserve completely gone, Funston betrayed the depression and sadness that were filling his heart at this point:

> I can't make new chums [,] because I have gone past that period in my life when I can make new friendships and I tell you it would take a mighty fine man to occupy one small

corner of Franklin's [E. C. Franklin had recently married.]
part of my heart. I tell you, old man, I am beginning to feel
pretty sore about those things [separation from old friends]
and to see that I am tsoon [sic] be alone in the world.
. . .Yesterday I thought of this so hard that I shed some
unmanly tears, . . .The best of my life is behind me. Nothing
can ever occur that can make me thoroughly happy, this is I
mean absolutely happy, but there can come about plenty of
hard luck, disappointments and heartaches. Would it be such
an awful thing after a [sic] if I met the fate of my predessor
[sic] [Major W. D.] Osgood, who in half a second went from
the full vigor of manhood into Eternity. [sic] [7]

Such thoughts of loneliness, misfortune, and death
portrayed the feelings of a man who had received his fill
of combat, courageous and able soldier though he was.
Warfare had continued all through these discouraging
first weeks of 1897, and its fortunes had been something else that contributed to Funston's growing revul-
sion toward his life as an *insurrecto* artilleryman. One of
the larger actions of this period was the fight that had
for a time marked the end to small-scale guerrilla activities. This fight began with a salvo from Funston's gun at
6 A.M. on March 13, 1897. The site of the conflict was
the fortified town of *Jiguani*, a Spanish outpost that was
situated in the *Bayamo* District of *Oriente* Province.
Since he had ravaged the countryside bare of edibles,
Garcia was desperate for a victory in this siege. If he
succeeded, Garcia anticipated that he could open bulg-
ing Spanish warehouses and feed and clothe his 4,000
emaciated troops properly for a time.

[7] Frederick Funston to Charles F. Scott, May 10, 1897, In Camp, Head-
quarters, Department of *Oriente*, near *Mejia*, Cuba, F. Funston Papers, Box
75; Frederick Funston to E. H. Funston, March 5, 1897, In Camp,
Headquarters, Department of *Oriente*, Cuba, F. Funston Papers, Box 75;
Frederick Funston to Ella Funston, May 10, 1897, In Camp, Headquarters,
Department of *Oriente*, near *Mejia*, Cuba, F. Funston Papers, Box 75;
Frederick Funston to Frank Webster, April 10, 1897, In Camp, Head-
quarters, Department of *Oriente*, near *Holguin*, Cuba (Uncited Newspaper
Reprint), F. Funston Papers, Box 75.

For their own part, Funston and his officers, who by now had relinquished all hope of ever again seeing their homes, looked forward to assaulting *Jiguani* with subdued optimism. They held no doubts that their force would take the town, and Funston himself confidently believed that once the town had capitulated, he would "probably be promoted to Lieut.-Colonel [sic]." Moreover, jaded with the war though they were, the major and his gunnery officers still took pride in their skill as artillerymen. What accounted for this professional spirit in large measure was the fact that the group was now quite satisfied with their weaponry. Funston's unit had just received an important delivery from the surreptitious supply system of the filibusters. This item was a long-barrel, twelve-pounder. It was a Driggs-Schroeder naval gun that was able to fire high-velocity, fixed rounds. Affectionately Hispanosizing this prized weapon, the Cubans dubbed the mule-borne, breech-firing piece *"Cayo Hueso"* in honor of its purchase site at Key West, Florida. Funston recognized that he critically needed this latest modern artillery instrument when he considered the task that was now before him at *Jiguani.*

In normal times an important commercial center, *Jiguani* was the largest town that the Cubans under Garcia's leadership had thus far tried to seize. In addition, its 800-man garrison, aside from the usual infantry elements, included cavalry and artillery contingents. This strong Spanish command also held the usual advantages in the form of impressive fortifications of blockhouses, trenches, and barbed-wire. When he surveyed the town's defenses, Funston concluded that *"El Castillo,"* a stone fort that sat astride a low hill that rose eighty feet above the main street, was the salient feature. *El Castillo's* collapse would mean a Spanish defeat. He decided, therefore, that he would personally direct *Cayo Hueso* and his older Hotchkiss twelve-pounder against *El Castillo*. He installed the two guns on a ridge that was 800 yards to the Northwest of the bastion. He ordered the crew of his remaining gun, a light two-pounder, to put their piece into position on *Jiguani's* southern edge. At sunrise, following Garcia's plan, Major Funston's batteries fired and initiated the siege.

Funston soon saw indications that this investment might not turn out successfully after all. For one thing, the fuses in the high-velocity rounds of *Cayo Hueso* proved too sensitive to be useful. They exploded before the warheads could make sufficient penetration of the walls of the Spanish fort and blow out chunks of the structure. For another thing, the old twelve-pounder, a hard-used veteran of many battles, went out of action early, because a defective shell failed to fire properly, and the warhead lodged in the barrel. Also, an ancient, eight-centimeter, Krupp field piece that the Spaniards had emplaced in an earthen fort adjacent to *El Castillo* began a gun-to-gun duel with *Cayo Hueso*. Funston was compelled by this development to concentrate the fire of his one working big gun in an effort to silence the enemy cannon. He had to knock out the enemy piece before he could shell any fortification.

One factor operated to Funston's advantage. Whenever it fired, the old-style, German-made cannon announced the propulsion of its round with a large puff of smoke that was visible for a considerable distance. Also, the Krupp's low-speed projectile was easily discernible by those who were its targets as it made its way to them. Funston and his gunners at once noted these obsolescent characteristics of the enemy's gun, and, taking advantage of the old Krupp's shortcomings, they played a kind of game with the crew of the enemy weapon. They watched the parapet of the Spanish emplacement for the tell-tale smoke; next, they searched out the slow-moving round and jumped from behind their guns whenever a direct hit looked probable; they ducked and waited a couple of seconds for the enemy round to explode; then, they rushed to the breech block of *Cayo Hueso* to fire a return shot. This "shoot-out" continued for several minutes until Funston and his gun crew succeeded in putting a disabling round into the Krupp's position.

Funston then turned loose *Cayo Hueso* on the key stronghold and other Spanish works as well. In a few minutes, he forced the evacuation of several trenches by the Spaniards. Next, he systematically destroyed one corner of *El Castillo* and thus exposed some of the vulnerable interior of the fort to the fire of the Cubans' small arms. At this point, the *expedicionario* major believed that the time was ripe for an assault, and he pressed Calixto Garcia to order a general infantry attack.

General Garcia, who did not wish to rush his troops into the deadly rounds of his own artillery that might fall short, decided to be cautious and wait for darkness. Also, Garcia had another reason for his hesitance to order an infantry advance at once. The seasoned *insurrecto* leader feared the confusion that might result among his troops should he countermand the orders for a night assault that he had already given by issuing a fresh and completely unanticipated verdict for an immediate assault. Funston dutifully acquiesced in the face of his superior's wishes. Yet, he thought that this failure to grab such a juicy opportunity had been a grave error. In consequence, he could reconcile himself to it only by believing that it was but one of many errors that battle-field commanders commonly made in such situations.

The siege continued, and Funston returned to his position on the ridge. Since there was no great amount of artillery activity, he took his ease behind a shade tree. The location was a dangerous one, because a Mauser bullet whizzed through the trunk and narrowly missed his chest. He had little time to mull over this particular scrape with death, however. The Spanish artillerymen had repaired their emplacement, and they now began to fire the vintage Krupp anew. Once again, Funston and his crew played "the artillery dance" with the Spanish cannoneers, though this time, they were not able to silence the persistent old weapon. Funston "was slightly wounded" by one of the Krupp's rounds when he failed to move to cover quickly enough. Fortunately, the momentum of the shell fragment that struck him in the chest was mostly spent. The "ugly piece of iron" that Funston picked up as a battle memento only knocked him off his feet and left "a bad bruise" whose traces disappeared in a week. Ultimately nightfall brought a temporary end to the artillery duel and gave an aching Funston some rest.

There was no time for real recuperation, however, for darkness also precipitated the Cuban infantry attack that Garcia had scheduled. At 9 P.M., Funston followed his orders and signaled the start of the attack by hurling a round from *Cayo Hueso* against the battered, but enduring, *El Castillo*. The Cubans staunchly moved forward, but the Spaniards, who had taken the precaution of reinforcing their shell-marred, ridgeline trenches during the early darkness, put up a stiff resistance. Consequently, the left wing of the Cubans' skirmish line came under heavy rifle fire, and they could not advance, although the right wing did make some progress. Its units seized posts that were within 200 yards of *El Castillo's* trenches. These *insurrectos* held the conquered positions for seven hours during the night before they retired to avoid being cut off by a possible Spanish counterattack at daylight.

It was during these hours of the right wing's precarious hold on the enemy's position that Funston, who felt that the tide of battle was running against the *insurrectos*, proposed two bold schemes to Garcia. First, taking his cue from what two *expeditionarios* had earlier done during a siege, he asked permission to lead his officers, who would be armed only with pistols, a crowbar, and twenty-five pounds of dynamite, to *El Castillo's* walls under the cover of darkness. The plan was to make a breech for the explosives, set off the deadly material, raise a general din, and then tell the Spanish garrison that they were confronted by a force of fifty men who were carrying additional charges and were fully ready to blow their position to pieces. Basing his plan on this ruse's previous success, Funston believed that his daring group could panic the Spaniards into surrendering their main defenses and thus revive the Cubans' waning fortunes at one swoop.

However, General Garcia, who was appalled by the idea of risking his entire contingent of artillery officers, refused Funston's plea. In consequence, Funston immediately proffered a second plan that involved only himself. He suggested that the general dispense with the pending two-sided bombardment that was then scheduled by him to commence at dawn and herald another *insurrecto* assault. Rather, Funston wished Garcia to let him make "a fire ball of cotton camphor and [gun] powder," and then allow him personally to ease the explosive combination through the night to the base of *El Castillo*. Once he was in the proper location, Funston planned to light the volatile mass. His intent then was to hurl it against the fortress' wall simultaneously with a sudden, rapid, concentrated barrage of all three artillery guns against the Spanish position. His hope was that the confused Spaniards would panic, think themselves on the verge of being overrun by stealthy Cuban infantry, and quit their strong post. Once more, however, Garcia's caution thwarted a Funston plan, and Funston, who was quite disappointed and believed that victory was slipping away, returned dejectedly to his guns to prepare for the next day's fighting.

Funston's feelings of pessimism were well founded as the events of March 14, 1897, the second day of the siege of *Jiguani*, demonstrated. Funston received the first serious combat wound of his Cuban service. The blow was struck by a fragment of Spanish shell that came from a missile of that persistent enemy, the redoubtable old Krupp gun. The jagged hot metal shredded his left arm, broke a bone, and left the appendage dangling at his side.

As on the previous day, perhaps because of his exhaustion, he had failed to take shelter quickly enough. He was directing his guns during the attack, and, when he saw "a dark object" coming at him, he "involuntarily" threw up his hands to cover his eyes. "A dull explosion" followed, and he was aware that his left arm was "mangled." Since he had no replacement, he received only the barest first aid, and he had to wait an hour for "a substitute" before he retired to the rear where he was able to get serious treatment. Subsequently, with his left arm wrapped in bandages and tied across his side and chest, he returned to his post and continued directing his three guns.

Also, Garcia started thinking of a withdrawal from *Jiguani*. The general was discouraged over the failure of his infantry attack of the preceding evening and disheartened by the Spaniards' continued stubborn resistance. In addition, as the fighting progressed, the *insurrectos* began to run short of ammunition. The last demoralizing development came when Garcia received alarming news from his scouts. A Spanish column that was last reported by *insurrecto* scouts to be near *Bayamo* now was possibly close enough to make a forced march and relieve *Jiguani* within a few hours.

Galvanized by this disconcerting intelligence into making a decision, General Garcia concluded to quit *Jiguani*. At once, he called off the attack, precipitously abandoned the investment, and hastily left the vicinity of the town. He had lost 400 men in the abortive assault and had pushed his jaded, hungry command hard. Moreover, much to the Cubans' chagrin, the scouts' information proved false later.

For his own part, Funston, who was completely tired out and whose arm was throbbing in pain, thought that he had learned another hard lesson in the art of war. He concluded that a commander who acted rashly on the basis of incomplete intelligence reports erred grievously. Such precipitous action could bring about a retreat that was not otherwise called for and such a development could shatter troops' morale and be more damaging to an army than an outright defeat.

Following his reverse at *Jiguani*, Garcia praised Funston and his artillerymen for their work in the siege and extended them a month's leave. The general, who was still feeling the impact of Captain-General Weyler's strategy, was short on supplies and munitions. Therefore, he was once more breaking up his army into numerous, smaller forces who could harass the Spaniards at every turn and try to live off the land. He foresaw no immediate need for his cannoneers, especially since they were exhausted and their guns lacked shells.

Actually, the veteran rebel *jefe* was again embarking upon the policy of keeping the insurrection alive by resorting to low-intensity guerrilla warfare. In the following weeks, General Garcia did in fact make it impossible for Weyler's troops who occupied the territory that was to the East of the *Cuato* River to move outside their fortified towns easily. He forced the Spaniards to be extremely cautious and to sally out of their forts only in strong columns, and these elements were easily assailable by the *insurrectos'* hit-and-run tactics. These enemy formations were cumbersome; they were road bound; and always, by necessity, they were accompanied by large parties of heavily-armed, well-mounted, pro-Spanish Cuban *guerrilleros*, and the behavior of these loyalists toward their compatriots only further enraged most native islanders and stiffened their will to resist Spanish rule.

During the first days of this renewed mobile warfare, Funston was on the northern coast of eastern Cuba

where Garcia had instructed him to spend his leave with
his fellow artillerymen. The general intended to put his
gunnery officers into new clothes, and, to that end, he
had given Funston $25.00. Every other officer had
received $20.00. Garcia put them in touch with one of
his agents along the coast. It was at this point, in
mid-March, 1897, that Funston finally discarded his be-
grimmed hunting jacket and corduroy trousers and
donned *insurrecto* cotton ducking for good. Funston
also persuaded Garcia to send out to the United States
Arthur R. Joyce, an artilleryman from Connecticut.
Joyce's mission was to procure a supply of more dependable shells from the *junta's* munitions manufacturers.[8]

Funston and the gunnery officers who remained
with him did not get to complete their month's leave.
An unexpected development caused Garcia to recall
them to duty late in March, 1897. The general received
word that the filibustering steamship *Laura* that was
carrying the expedition of Carlos Roloff, a veteran
blockade-runner, and considerable materiel had landed
on the coast at a point that was six miles from the town
of *Veguitas* on the Bay of *Banes*. At once Garcia assembled 4,000 men and all of the artillery of his scattered command and rapidly marched to the Bay. His
purpose was to fend off the Spanish, because they were

---

[8] A. Prats-Lerma, "La Actuacion del Teniente Coronel Frederick Funston,"
*Boletin del Ejercito*, Nov.-Dec., 1931, p. 366; Anonymous Newspaper
Article, Topeka, Kansas, *Daily Capital*, March [?], 1898, F. Funston
Papers, Box 75; Anonymous Newspaper Interview, Topeka, Kansas, *Daily
Capital*, January 12, 1898, F. Funston Papers, Box 75; Arthur Royal
Joyce, Untitled and Uncited Article, October 29, 1917, F. Funston Papers,
Box 75; Charles F. Scott, "Frederick Funston," *The Independent*, April
11, 1901, p. 820; Frederick Funston, "A Defeat and A Victory," *Scrib-
ner's Magazine*, December, 1910, pp. 736-755; "Frederick Funston,"
*Harper's Weekly*, March 5, 1898, p. 226; Frederick Funston to Charles F.
Scott, August 31, 1897, *Victoria de Las Tunas, Oriente* Province, Cuba, F.
Funston Papers, Box 75; Frederick Funston to E. H. Funston, March 5,
1897, *ibid.*; Frederick Funston to Ella Funston, May 10, 1897, *ibid.*;
Kansas City, Missouri, *Times,* January 14, 1936, Section D, p. 16, c. 3-4.

rushing into the area over 3,000 men in three separate columns. They were also marshalling several ships and concentrating them about the Bay in order to trap the expedition and destroy its supplies.

In the ensuing action, Funston took part in a heavy exchange of fire that developed between Cubans who were ashore and Spaniards who were aboard the gunboat *Jorge Juan* in the Bay of *Banes*. Other Spanish gunboats also moved onto the scene. These warships were convoying troop transports that were carrying 3,000 additional infantrymen whose intent was to land on the beach and aid their comrades who were pressing the Cubans from the interior. In an effort to strike at these warships, Funston experienced an unusual martial event. He was a member of the rebel party of sappers who successfully mined and blew up one of the smaller gunboats, destroying the vessel and its entire crew. With the same group of demolition experts, Funston joined in a second attempt at mining Spanish craft. This time the target was a troopship that the party intended to sink at the mouth of the Bay and so deny the anchorage to the Spaniards. Unfortunately for the Cubans, the scheme failed.

Funston's other battle experiences during these days of hard fighting around the Bay of *Banes* stemmed from more conventional land activities. These operations were characterized by success. Funston fought hard with Garcia's troops in the running fight that the Cubans waged against the Spaniards who were menacing Roloff from the interior side of the Bay of *Banes*. This occurred when the Cubans, who had already repulsed the Spanish amphibious attack on Roloff, turned inland. The *insurrectos* were attempting to check the powerful Spanish columns that were driving to the Bay in order to smash the expedition before it left the beach. Funston's artillery formed a key part of the Cubans' defense, and his field guns inflicted over fifty casualties upon the ene-

my. At one point, Funston's artillery pieces put down a
heavy barrage and helped to prevent the Spaniards'
encirclement of Garcia. By this energetic operation, the
Cubans finally discouraged the Spanish, who withdrew
and allowed the Roloff expedition to move safely into
the interior and deliver their critical supplies to the
*insurrectos*.

Funston's next sizeable encounter occurred in early
May, 1897, several days after the furious fighting
around the Bay of *Banes* had ended. Garcia, who was
again dispersing his command in order to harry Spanish
outposts, detached the artillerist and some of his cannoneers from his personal command. The general sent
them to support the activities of one of his subordinate
*insurrecto* units. Funston's new commander, who saw
that his reinforcing gunners were using a newly-arrived,
Hotchkiss twelve-pounder, decided to bombard the port
city of *Sama*. This community was Spanish-occupied,
and it sat on the northern coast at a point that was
seventeen miles from *Veguitas*. On the morning of May
9, Funston's artillery unit and an escort of Cuban foot
troops began a difficult two-day march. The column
moved through a forest that was so dense that the men
had no choice but to cut their own trail through the
heavy brush and timber.

The hours of tough hacking paid off. As darkness
fell on May 10, 1897, the men went into camp on the
reverse slope of a hill that overlooked *Sama*. When they
had light enough very early the next day, they dug a
long trench that ran along the forward crest of one of
the heights and made preparations to attack. Funston
and his crew, who were most eager to try the new gun,
hauled the Hotchkiss into firing position, and, at daybreak on May 11, they announced the start of the
combat by firing a round at the Spaniards. Funston
directed this initial bombardment at a small wooden
fort that lay eight hundred yards downslope, and the

cannon's first missile hit the target squarely. The Spaniards immediately returned a heavy fire from their numerous blockhouses that ringed the port.

After Funston and his crew had fired only five rounds, the Hotchkiss was disabled by a Spanish hit that broke the axle. Funston saw that he could not fire the weapon again without making repairs and that he could not repair the damage on the spot. Thoroughly chagrined, Funston ordered his men to haul the indespensible gun to the nearest rebel facility. Since this shop lay in a protected camp that was thirty miles away, Funston took part in no more action at *Sama*. The entire besieging force, in fact, might also have done well to withdraw at this point. The capture of a few cattle, the seizure of several horses, and the burning of some out · buildings were the only accomplishments of this four-day event. To Funston the whole operation seemed "disastrous," and its outcome was indeed portentious, since equally frustrating times lay just ahead for Funston and his comrades.[9]

[9] A. Prats-Lerma, "La Actuacion del Teniente Coronel Frederick Funston," *Boletin del Ejercito*, Nov.-Dec., 1931, pp. 365-366; Emory W. Fenn, "Ten Months with the Cuban Insurgents," *Century*, June, 1898, p. 303-304; Frederick Funston, "A Defeat and A Victory," *ibid.*, pp. 741-742; "Frederick Funston," *ibid.*

# 8

## Hard Times and a Victory for *Cuba Libre*

The fruitless venture at *Sama* was just the beginning of a
period of disappointment and suffering for Funston and
his colleagues. During the warm, rainy weeks of the
spring and summer of 1897, the fortunes of the Cuban
cause ebbed low. In this steamy interval, Garcia continued his dispersed brand of guerrilla warfare, and
Funston found himself involved in a military pattern
that alternated between foraging for food and participating in one of the numerous "pin-prick attacks" that
Garcia's men staged against Spanish posts and columns.

Then, in a scrape with the enemy on June 20,
Funston sustained a severe wound that almost killed
him. He "was shot through the body, the [Mauser rifle]
ball piercing both lungs and missing . . . [his] heart a
scant three-quarters of an inch." The Spanish bullet
fortunately only cut through "the apex of Funston's
heart." Although it passed entirely through Funston and
then killed a Cuban who was taking refuge behind a tree
trunk, the slug did not "flatten and shatter." Unlike the
slower-moving, American-made, lead-nose Remington
bullets, the high-velocity, steel-jacketed Mauser missiles
left clean holes in their human targets, and thereby, in
spite of their striking power, they often facilitated recovery.

Funston's situation was grave and for the following
ten weeks, his life hung in the balance. Critically injured, he was in the charge of a medical detachment that
ran one of the *insurrectos'* poorly-equipped and under-

staffed hospitals. Funston's experiences as a casualty illustrated well just how thinly provided with some supplies and facilities the *insurrectos'* cause really was. After he had received first aid on the battlefield, Funston underwent a painful journey several miles through the forest. He traveled agonizingly slowly, because he was lying "in a hammock, [that was] hung from a long pole . . . carried by two big negro Revolutionists, . . ." In this primitive manner, he ultimately reached a remote "mountain hospital" where he began his excruciating and slow recovery. Aside from his wound, he—like all the other patients who were convalescing at the secret *insurrecto* installation—had to worry about the danger of discovery by the pro-Spanish, Cuban *guerrilleros.* These loyalists' special brutality was ferreting out and destroying *insurrecto* hospitals, without granting any quarter whatsoever.

Though these merciless royalists fortunately did not appear, Funston for a time still feared for his life. His natural healing powers were abysmally low because of the exhaustion that stemmed from his improper diet and months of arduous campaigning. Too, the inadequacies of the Cuban medical system further retarded his convalescence. Though he received the close attentions of his own personal, partially-trained, male nurse—his *"practicante"*—Funston needed expert medical care. Also, while the basic medicines and foodstuffs were plentiful enough, the hospital's arrangements were often unsanitary. Funston contracted typhoid fever as he lay recuperating in his bull-hide hammock. This ailment further weakened him and delayed the complete healing of his lung wound. Indeed, months later, after he had returned to Kansas, he still was going through fits of coughing and spitting up blood.[1]

[1] Charles F. Scott, "Frederick Funston," *The Independent,* April 11, 1901, p. 820; C. S. Gleed, "Romance and Reality," *Cosmopolitan,* July, 1899, p. 327; Emory W. Fenn, "Ten Months with the Cuban Insurgents," *Cen-*

In spite of his medical handicaps, Funston believed that he was fit enough for active duty by the latter part of August, 1897. Since the long-planned fall offensive of General Garcia was approaching, he did not have to await his chief's orders for long. Garcia sent out word for his command to reconcentrate near the heavily fortified town of *Victoria de las Tunas*, a place that was known to the Cubans simply as *"Las Tunas."* This Spanish-held center was situated in northern *Oriente* Province, and it was adjacent to the boundary of *Camaguey* Province. This Spanish outpost was the next objective of the eastern department's leader.

Laying siege to *Las Tunas* was a gigantic undertaking for the Cubans. The Spanish commander of the bastion controlled a garrison that consisted of 800 infantrymen, forty-seven Cuban loyalists—the hated *guerrilleros*—and a unit of artillerymen, whose weapons were two Krupp field guns. The fortifications that were defended by this

*tury,* June, 1898, p. 306; Frederick Funston to Charles F. Scott, August 31, 1897, *Victoria de Las Tunas, Oriente* Province, Cuba, F. Funston Papers, Box 75; Untitled Newspaper Articles, Kansas City, Missouri, *Journal,* February 25, 1917, no page number, in *Frederick Funston, Clippings, Volume I, K.S.H.S.*; William Allen White, *Autobiography*, p. 306; William Henry Sears to R. J. Oulahan, February 27, 1917, Washington, D.C., William Henry Sears Papers, *Kansas State Historical Society*, Topeka, Kansas; Sears was one of Funston's friends who lived at Lawrence, Kansas; he talked at length with Funston at some point in May or June, 1898, during a meeting with the former artilleryman in Lawrence; there was some confusion in regard to the time and place of Funston's receiving his bad lung wound; see the Topeka, Kansas, *Daily Capital,* January 12, 1898, and later in early March [?], 1898, in Funston Papers, Box 75, and the letter of Charles A. Arand to the *Kansas State Historical Society*, on September 25, 1936, from Sault Ste. Marie, Michigan. Arand's letter enclosed a handbill that advertised one of Funston's lectures in Kansas about Cuba in April, 1898. The handbill proclaimed that Funston was "desperately wounded" at "Monte Alto Sama." The two newspapers claimed that the lung wound occurred at *Sama,* a battle that Funston fought on May 11, 1897. In his correspondence and *Scribner's* articles, Funston never mentioned *Monte Alto*; he never wrote of his wounding at *Sama*; rather, he wrote expressly to Charles F. Scott on August 31, 1897, that he took his lung shot in a battle that occured on June 20, 1897; it would seem better to trust Funston's memory on this point.

sizeable medley of troops consisted of twenty-two loop-
holed and sandbagged strongpoints that were connected
by communications trenches and protected by barbed-
wire entanglements. Two of the strongest of these works
lay near the center of the town. One was a built-up
infantry barracks, and the other was a strengthened
cavalry barracks. Together, these two strongpoints created an "in-depth" defense for *Las Tunas.*

Counteracting somewhat this defensive strength of
the Spanish were several fortuitous factors that worked
in behalf of Gracia's Cubans. One of these was geographical in nature. *Las Tunas* sat on an open plain that, along
its southern edge, underlay a low ridge. Funston, who
had by now perfected his artilleryman's *coup d'oeil,*
realized at once that this elevated mass held great importance. He concluded that the ridge was a perfect position for his artillery, because the height would enable
his main guns to enfilade the Spaniards' key defenses.
Gracia approved Funston's plan for deployment of the
guns on the ridge.

Another factor that favored the Cubans was basic-
ally military in nature. For once, the attacking Cubans
were able to amass preponderant strength in both men
and guns. Garcia had put together a force of almost
6,000 men. This aggregation was large enough both to
let Garcia invest the garrison and seal off *Las Tunas*
from any relief from the outside. Accordingly, the general made lavish deployments. He ordered one 2,000-
man force to block the road that ran to the South
toward *Bayamo.* He designated another 2,000-man unit
to close the road that headed to the East toward *Holguin.* When he had these dispositions done, the mous-
tached veteran still retained a body of nearly 2,000
assault troops to throw against the town.

In addition, the Cuban wealth in numbers was for
once relatively well matched by the Cuban strength in
artillery. Funston at last commanded what amounted to

a full battery of artillery, even though the guns were a motley assortment of calibers and makes. His arsenal still included *Cayo Hueso*, but it also sported two Hotchkiss twelve-pounders and a pair of Hotchkiss two-pounders. One of these twelve-pounders was a piece that had been brought in by the Roloff Expedition, and it was yet untested by combat. A French *expedicionario* failed to operate the new weapon effectively and missed a practice target on several successive tries. So, Garcia ordered Funston, who had just arrived at the army's assembly camp, to test-fire the new gun. Funston did so right away, and he hit the mark repeatedly, proving to his comrades that his severe wound had not diminished his artillery skills.

Aside from this new piece of traditional military hardware, there was something else now at Funston's disposal that was a novelty. The major's assemblage of firepower incorporated a strange, new instrument of destruction that already enjoyed a dreaded reputation. Also smuggled by the rebels into Cuba on the Roloff Expedition, this weapon was a Sims-Dudley dynamite gun. It was the tube-like device that Funston had encountered during the artillery practice firing that had occurred on Long Island a year earlier.[2]

The way in which the dynamite gun functioned fascinated Funston, who was the first man ever to use it in warfare. He noted that the weapon's ten-pound projectile was really a brass cylinder. This can-like container measured a foot and a half in length and two inches in diameter, and it held five pounds of highly-explosive nitroglycerin. The discharge of a small amount of smokeless powder in one of the gun's two barrels com-

[2] A. Prats-Lerma, "La Actuacion del Teniente Coronel Frederick Funston," *Boletin del Ejercito*, Nov.-Dec., 1931, pp. 367-368; Emory W. Fenn, "Ten Months with the Cuban Insurgents," *ibid.*, pp. 305-306; Frederick Funston, "A Defeat and A Victory," *Scribner's Magazine*, December, 1910, pp. 742-743, 750-751.

pressed the air in the other barrel. It was the sudden release of this pent-up air that propelled the tubelike projectile toward the target at a slow, initial velocity of only 600 feet per second. Funston soon learned that any gunner who was firing at a distant object had to elevate the barrel considerably before he released the round. At *Las Tunas*, he discovered something else about the performance of the Sims-Dudley piece. While it was decidedly deadly when a gunner employed it against small, lightly-constructed blockhouses, the dynamite gun's effectiveness was mainly psychological when an artilleryman used it against massive fortifications. Upon detonation, the shells of the gun produced a terrible ear-rending noise that eventually unnerved defenders.

In spite of his curiosity to try out the new air-gun, Funston hesitated for a few moments when he prepared to bombard the Spanish with cylinders of dynamite for the first time at *Las Tunas*. He had only watched others fire the gun during the exercise on Long Island; he had never before actually discharged the dynamite-hurling piece. For two days prior to the siege, he had studiously pondered the book of instructions that had come with the Sims-Dudley, and, as a professional artilleryman, he was determined to douse the Spaniards with a new form of destruction.

There was something else behind Funston's resoluteness to use the unfamiliar gun, and this was a personal, psychological factor. The Kansan was resolved to demonstrate to his comrades that he harbored neither dismay nor fear of something that was new and allegedly quite formidable. Consequently, when the time arrived, Funston casually rolled out the piece, calmly sighted on his target, and—so it seemed to observers—confidently let go the first shot. Later, when he wrote of the event, he used humor and self-deprecation to cloak the fact that firing the unknown, fearsome gun

Funston fires the "dynamite gun" during the siege of *Victoria de Las Tunas.*

had required an exercise of courage, something that was Funston's forte:

> For a second she [the dynamite gun] seemed to wheeze; it's all up I thought; the Cubans ran; but I didn't dare to; it was only a second and then she coughed and the air in the Spanish fort was filled with misfit logs and debris; and I knew it was all right. I turned around and grinned like the cat that had swallowed the canary, and no one knew that I had just finished making four or five kinds of a fool of myself. After they had set 'em [sic] up in the other alley we rolled 'em [sic] again.[3]

Funston's recollection of the incident with the Sims-Dudley gun referred to an event that came at the beginning of the siege of *Las Tunas*, an operation that Garcia commenced early on August 28, 1897. Major Funston's guns opened the struggle by unleashing a salvo from their well-sited entrenchment. In a few hours, the three twelve-pounders and the dynamite launcher took a heavy toll at the Spaniards' expense. In spite of the loss of one twelve-pounder because of a malfunction, Funston's artillerists methodically blasted the Spanish defenses into smoking rubble.

Funston's gunners knocked out the outlying small forts; then they silenced the two Krupp guns and enfiladed the main trenches; and finally they even demolished several of the important large blockhouses. The Sims-Dudley did yeoman service in the hands of the Kansas major, who directed the new gun mainly against the smaller outposts and the trenchline.

Though he was quite busy with the artillery work, Funston nonetheless took the time to observe the fiercest infantry actions of the struggle at *Las Tunas*. He

---

[3] Frederick Funston, *ibid.*, pp. 743-744; William Allen White, "Gen. Frederick Funston," *Harper's Weekly*, May 20, 1899, p. 496; Louis S. Young and Henry D. Northrop, *Life and Heroic Deeds of Admiral Dewey*, pp. 346-347.

watched from his gun emplacement as the *insurrectos* stormed the fortified cavalry barracks. He was enthralled by the action at the scene that he termed "the grand feature of the siege." Funston concluded that what he had witnessed "was like the battles of the story books, and [that] it was worth years of hum-drum life to see it."

Further stirring to Funston's *Kiplingesque* strain was the battle death of his friend and fellow *expedicionario* from the United States, Louis Napoleon Chapleau. Shot in the neck while he was participating in the infantry assault on the cavalry barracks, Chapleau bled to death, since a Cuban surgeon was unable to staunch the severed artery soon enough. Funston, who was standing with Garcia and his staff, was by the side of the severely wounded man as he died, exclaiming, "It is finished! It is finished!" The episode touched Funston deeply, for he believed that it epitomized the nobility of a brave and honorable death in behalf of a worthy cause.

There was, as usual, no time for lengthy reflection on these events, and Funston soon returned to his guns. He controlled the close overhead fire support that fell only thirty yards ahead of the advancing Cuban infantry, who were engaged in storming the trenches that were near the conquered cavalry barracks. He subsequently undertook such other artillery tasks as the needs of battle dictated.

Then, on the second day of the siege of *Las Tunas*, Funston ordered a protracted—and seemingly futile—cannonade of the last remaining, major Spanish post, a redoubt that lay inside the thick-walled infantry barracks that the Spaniards called the *"Cuartel General."* After *Cayo Hueso's* numerous rounds had apparently failed to dent the Spaniards' resolve, Funston resorted to radically unorthodox methods. He ordered his artillerymen to bash their way through the walls of several blocks of adjacent stone buildings, and, thereby making use of excellent cover, he eased his guns up to within a few yards of the hold-out Spaniards. He positioned a Hotchkiss twelve-pounder and the dynamite gun together in a warehouse where their muzzles were within less than 150 yards of the shell-pocked bastion. There followed a large dose of close-range fire. Still, after several hours, the Spanish appeared undaunted. Consequently, at 10 P.M. Funston, who was completely drained physically, fell asleep. He lay down side by side with his men, and all were stretched out on the warehouse floor behind the guns.

Early the next morning, Funston, aided by a fellow *expedicionario* and several Cuban colleagues, ended the resistance. Funston and his comrades had heard from a captured Spaniard that the enlisted soldiers of the *Cuartel General* were demoralized by the heavy shelling and were ready to surrender. So, the artillerists embarked upon a bold bid for peace. Funston and several others walked out into the vacant street before the Spanish outpost, stood completely out in the open, and called for the enemy troops to give up their pointless fight.

After a time, still shouting out their pleas for honorable capitulation, Funston and his group made their way slowly toward the wicked-looking loopholes. Funston's tension mounted as he neared the Spanish barbed-wire, for he well knew that some nervous Spaniard might shoot. Fortunately, no one fired, and the Spanish soldiers, who directly disobeyed their officers, threw down their weapons and filed out to become prisoners. The nitroglycerin of the Sims-Dudley cylinders and the hammering of *Cayo Hueso's* shells had completely subverted even the most stubborn Spanish *soldado's* will to continue.

At this point, the siege was just about over, and Funston afterwards concerned himself with purely noncombatant activities. He was exhausted and had taken some bruising punishment during the siege's earlier phases. While he was standing on the parapet and calling the ranges out to his gunners during the first day of combat, Funston had sustained a minor wound. He was blown backwards several feet and knocked unconscious by the explosion of a shell that came from one of the enemy's Krupps. He received a slight shock from the concussion, and he was hit in the chest by a piece of rock that was thrown up by the detonation of the round. He had seen the muzzle flash, and he knew that the shell was on its way—the familiar gun game with the old-style Krupps was again going on. But, Funston was just too tired of jumping and running to go to any cover. So, this time he stood his ground. Luckily, there was no blood, just dull aches and soreness. After Colonel Carlos Garcia doused him with a bucket of dirty, cannon-swabbing water, Funston revived, and, an hour later, he was back upon the exposed parapet, estimating ranges and shouting, "*Viva Cuba libre!*"

During the late afternoon and evening of the second day's fighting, Funston underwent another physical agony. This piece of suffering was all too familiar to him by this time. He was prostrated by one of his recurring attacks of malaria. His temperature soared, and he sweated profusely. He became delirious, and he had to leave the lines and go to the rear, where he experienced the usual, teeth-rattling chill. The spell passed, and following some rest, he was with his guns again by 10 P.M.

Aside from his aches and malarial weakness, Funston was bothered by another bodily complaint. He was just plain hungry. Consequently, his immediate urge at the end of his biggest stationary action in Cuba was to eat. He was famished for ample quantities of good wholesome food, an item that really he had not taken for several days. Not surprisingly, he rushed into the Spanish officers' mess, seized some canned goods, and hacked them open with his machete. Then, he greedily threw himself upon some sausages and crudely devoured them, using his battered blade and dirty fingers to do so while an officer prisoner looked on in astonishment and disbelief.

His appetite somewhat appeased by the Spanish rations, Funston wandered outside to the street and became a shocked observer of one of the brutalities of the Cuban insurrection. He witnessed the victors' exacting vengeance on their vanquished countrymen, the despised, pro-Spanish Cuban *guerrilleros*. Because they were members of units that were well-known by the *insurrectos* to be guilty of merciless conduct in the past, these loyalists found that their request for honorable surrender had fallen on deaf ears. Consequently, the defeated men knew that they would receive from the *insurrectos* no quarter such as that which the surrendered Spanish regulars almost invariably got. Funston almost turned away from the subsequent scene. He saw the forty-odd Cuban guerrillas march calmly out of their position, drop their weapons, and wait placidly until the *insurrectos* fell upon them with their machetes and hacked them to a bloody death in retribution for like outrages.

Following this grisly event, Funston was keen for more pleasant things. He soon made congenial contacts with a group of captured Spanish officers, who showed great interest in the dynamite gun, and Funston gladly revealed its mysteries to them. These commissioned prisoners lavished praise on the rebels' artillery unit, and they understandably left Funston with a high regard for them as soldiers and men.

Funston found these Spaniards both amiable and sporting, and he was gratified to see his fellow insurgents march the captured officers and their men off safely for release at nearby Spanish garrisons. Generally, the Cubans allowed captured Spaniards to rejoin their forces, since, with their limited resources, the rebel elements had no means of caring for large numbers of prisoners. Funston thought that this *insurrecto* practice was generous indeed, for the Spanish crown did not recognize the paroles that the Spaniards gave to their rebel captors. Consequently, as the Cubans well knew, before long, many of their erstwhile prisoners would be in the field again and would be campaigning anew against the revolution.[4]

There was something that was far more pleasant for Funston to contemplate than the *insurrectos'* policy toward Spanish prisoners. This element was the tremendous significance of the rebels' victory at *Las Tunas*. While he recognized the importance of the outcome of the siege psychologically in raising the Cubans' morale, Funston saw another meaning in the conquest of the town—the *insurrectos* could fight like regular troops and do so well. The Spaniards' loss of 40 percent of their garrison and twenty-one of their forts showed this fact clearly. Funston believed that the siege was the best military work and the "biggest victory" that Cubans had ever achieved on the island—either in the present rebellion or in that of "the Ten Years' War" a generation earlier. In his opinion, the *insurrectos* "had gone at the thing right, pressed every advantage, hung on like grim death, and made no serious mistakes."

Funston also thought that the booty that had been captured by the rebels in the three days and two nights of fighting was an impressive indication of a successful martial endeavor. Two Krupp field pieces, 1,150 Mauser rifles, over one million rounds of small arms ammuni-

---

[4] A. Prats-Lerma, "La Actuacion del Teniente Coronel Frederick Funston," *Boletin del Ejercito*, Nov.-Dec., 1931, pp. 367-369; Frederick Funston, *ibid.*, pp. 744-754; Frederick Funston to Charles F. Scott, August 31, 1897, *Victoria de Las Tunas, Oriente* Province, Cuba, F. Funston Papers, Box 75; the New York *Times*, April 30, 1899, p. 6, c. 5-6; William H. Sears to Richard J. Oulahan, February 27, 1917, Lawrence, Kansas, William Henry Sears Papers. *Kansas State Historical Society*, Topeka, Kansas.

tion, and well over two hundred prisoners were, so he concluded, ample material evidence of the triumph. It was no surprise that the exultant Cubans believed that the victory at *Las Tunas* had won the war for them.

In addition, it pleased Funston to note two other post-battle facts. First, the determined *insurrectos* had turned back a Spanish relief column that tried to lift the siege. Second, the fairly high cost of this "fearfully bloody affair" had not deterred Garcia and his men from pursuing their goal. They had lost 106 men, killed and wounded, and about one half of these casualties were officers. This high rate of officer loss was keenly felt by Funston, who counted two killed and three wounded from his nine-man stable of commissioned gunners; and, also, he reckoned that half of the Cuban infantry that were supporting his artillery had fallen. Indeed, given these losses and the accomplishments of the guns, Funston felt soldierly pride in what his unit had contributed to the victory. So did the Cubans. The artillerymen, in fact, became "the heroes of the day," and nothing was too good for them. And, now for a change, Funston came to believe that the Cuban cause had reason for some optimism after all.[5]

Reflecting this general Cuban esteem of the artillery, Garcia raised each artillery officer one full rank. On August 30, 1897, Funston became a Lieutenant-Colonel of the Cuban Liberation Army, the highest grade that he attained during his island tour with the *insurrectos*.

Funston and his fellow North Americans, who were flushed with victory and felt genuinely benign, reciprocated the Cubans' good will. They took advantage of this ebullient, postsiege spirit to seek another favor from their commander. Funston headed the *expedicionario*

---

[5] Emory W. Fenn, "Ten Months with the Cuban Insurgents," *Century* June, 1898, p. 306; Frederick Funston, "A Defeat and A Victory," *ibid.*, p. 753; Frederick Funston to Charles F. Scott, August 31, 1897, *ibid.*

group who petitioned Garcia to elevate the Negro first-sergeant of the artillery's infantry support unit to officer rank. The Kansan and his men understood that the Cuban leader, though he was desirous of recognizing the black soldier's abilities by a promotion, had long shunned the move because of the *expedicionarios'* supposed attitude. Garcia had feared that the North American whites' reputed disinclination to serve directly with black officers might bring damaging disharmony to his command. Funston, however, assuaged this apprehension when he presented the petition to Garcia, who was happy to comply with the request.

Funston personally took the able black sergeant his commission as second lieutenant. Though it was perhaps a patronizing gesture in the light of the racial views that many North Americans would hold seventy-five years later, Funston's action was not ungenerous at that time. In view of the intensity and pervasiveness of the North American racial prejudice at the turn of the century, Garcia's fear was well-grounded. Funston felt that he had done something extraordinary and gracious for a white American, and the episode was one of his happier Cuban memories.[6]

---

[6] "Cuban and Philippine Island Documents," F. Funston Papers, Box 76; Frederick Funston, "A Defeat and A Victory," *ibid.*, p. 754; "Frederick Funston," *Harper's Weekly*, March 5, 1898, p. 226; Frederick Funston to Charles F. Scott, August 31, 1897, *ibid.*; Funston failed to name this black Cuban soldier.

# 9

## The Clouded Departure

Aside from the satisfaction that he felt about having done his job well and the pride that he took in his promotion, Funston looked upon the siege at *Las Tunas* as a significant event in another very important way. He fully intended that the bloody affair would be his last major Cuban combat. Glory and adventure could only go so far in compensating him for the rigors of his life as an *insurrecto* in the field, and, as September, 1897, arrived, Funston concluded that his health was completely "broken down by the hardships that . . . [he had] undergone . . ." He still remained ardent for the rebel cause, and he heartily disliked the thought of quitting before the war ended. Yet, as he had indicated in a letter to his sister during the previous spring, he was ready to go home once the fall came. Reluctantly, Funston had finally decided that Cuba was among those tropical "yellow legged countries . . . [that were] frauds when it . . . [came] to staying too long in them."[1]

Funston dallied awhile longer, partly because Garcia had asked him to stay, and partly because he simply detested the idea of leaving his comrades in Cuba to fight on without him. While he remained a somewhat reluctant member of Garcia's command during September, 1897, he was involved in several small-scale brushes with the Spaniards. Then, as these actions continued

---

[1] Frederick Funston to Charles F. Scott, August 31, 1897, *Victoria de Las Tunas, Oriente* Province, Cuba, F. Funston Papers, Box 75.

into October, Funston sustained his third and last
wound as an *insurrecto* fighter. While he was participating in a running cavalry fight, he was thrown down hard
upon the ground by his horse that the pursuing Spaniards had shot from under him. Killed immediately by
the enemy's bullets, the animal suddenly became a mass
of dead weight possessing much momentum. He tossed
over Funston as though he were a leaf, and then he
rolled atop the prostrate Kansan's lower portions, crush-
ing both his legs. Funston's left leg took the worse
pounding, since the inert bulk of the horse badly
bruised the hip bone and drove the splintered end of a
dry stick onto which Funston had fallen deep into the
flesh of the upper leg. The *insurrectos* removed Funston
safely from the battlefield and again placed him in a
secluded *insurrecto* hospital.

When he had the time to assess his situation anew,
Funston found that his healing powers were still quite
inadequate. His left hip and thigh pained him constantly, and, worse, they refused to heal properly. Before
long, "an obstinate abscess" developed inside the wound
that had been caused by the stick. Funston realized that
he was now running the danger of developing an infec-
tion that well might kill him. In addition, he was, as he
continued to do for months afterwards, walking with a
decided limp, since his left leg could not support his
weight at all well while he was on his feet, even for a
limited time. For all practical purposes, Funston considered himself an invalid who was entirely unfit for
military service when November, 1897, rolled around.
Consequently, he now firmly resolved to return home at
once in order to obtain proper care and rest before he
either died or became a permanent cripple.[2]

---

[2] Charles F. Scott, "Frederick Funston," *The Independent*, April 11, 1901,
p. 820; C. S. Gleed, "Romance and Reality," *Cosmopolitan*, July, 1899,
pp. 327-328; "Funston and Pershing," New York *Evening Post*, May 9,

Such a painful and lingering hip injury by no means cut short the career of an *insurrecto* who had yet to prove himself in battle and establish a reputation as a capable soldier fighting in the cause of a *Cuba libre*. Funston had long ago attained those things. He had been engaged "in more that 20 battles," not counting the small, short-lived encounters, during the fifteen months that preceded his third wounding. Those Cubans who had served with the artillery chief admired his abilities both as a tactician and as an organizer. They regarded him affectionately as *muy simpatico* and *muy bravo*—as a true friend of Cuban independence and as a soldier who was completely fearless in fighting the enemy. Funston's image among his fellow *insurrectos*, in fact, was that of "a perfect daredevil" whose comrades would follow him anywhere to try anything at any time. Even the Spaniards—as they indicated later—were laudatory of the "little American that used to handle Gomez's artillery." In their eyes, he was "the little devil [who] hauled his guns up so close [to our defensive positions] that they scorched our eyebrows." Funston was well aware of his standing as a respected *expedicionario* fighter, and he had no reason by November, 1897, to think that he had not done his full measure for the islanders' cause.[3]

1916, no page number, John J. Pershing Papers, Box 383, *Scrapbook*, pp. 187-188, Mss. Division, The Library of Congress, Washington, D. C.; F. F. Eckdall, "'Fighting' Fred Funston," Speech in the *Kansas State Historical Quarterly*, Spring, 1956, p. 81; Frederick Funston to Frank Webster, January 14, 1898, New York City, New York (Reprinted in Topeka, Kansas, *Daily Capital*, January 19, 1898), F. Funston Papers, Box 75; Louis S. Young and Henry D. Northrop, *Life and Heroic Deeds of Admiral Dewey*, p. 347; Untitled Newspaper Article, the Kansas City, Missouri, *Times*, January 14, 1936, Section D, p. 16, c. 3-4; Untitled Newspaper Interview, the Topeka, Kansas, *Daily Capital*, January 12, 1898, F. Funston Papers, Box 75.

[3] A. Prats-Lerma, "La Actuacion del Teniente Coronel Frederick Funston," *Boletin del Ejercito*, Nov.-Dec., 1931, p. 377; Charles F. Scott, *ibid.*, pp. 819-820; C. S. Gleed, *ibid.*; "Frederick Funston," *Harper's Weekly*, March

Also, there was a personal and psychological reason why the physically depleted Funston could believe that he had accomplished his task and could now accept the necessity of quitting Cuba. Part of his motivation for coming into the insurrection in the first place had stemmed from his view of the nature and significance of war. Both Funston's family background and his wide reading of history, heroic fiction, and poetry had given him his particular attitude toward war. To Funston, military combat was an exciting, romantic adventure in which a participant could prove that he possessed all of the admirable and desirable virile qualities—courage, tenacity, loyalty, resourcefulness, honesty, and—perhaps above all—an unflinching acceptance of death. This last soldierly virtue involved dealing out death as much as it did calmly taking its arrival. With this quality—just as with the others—Funston felt that he had fulfilled his expectations, for he had killed at least thirteen men in Cuba for certain. He knew, because he had shot them, and afterwards he had seen their bodies.

Significantly, Funston remembered vividly the two occasions on which he had personally slain his enemies and subsequently viewed the carnage that his own hand had wrought. One of these events occurred while Funston was mounted and foraging for food alone. Taken by surprise, Funston was cut off from his men by a squad of seven Spanish cavalrymen, who put him under a heavy fusillade and chased him into a patch of woods. Abandoning his horse in panic, he took refuge amidst the foliage and lay very still. Finally, after he had chastised himself for his cowardice and remembered his prowess as a Kansas squirrel hunter, he regained his

5, 1898, p. 226; James W. Wadsworth, Jr., *The Autobiography of James W. Wadsworth, Jr.*, pp. 48-50, James W. Wadsworth, Jr., Papers, "Diaries, Autobiography," Box 15, Mss. Division, the Library of Congress, Washington, D. C.; William H. Sears to Richard J. Oulahan, February 27, 1917, Washington, D. C., William H. Sears Papers, *Kansas State Historical Society*, Topeka, Kansas.

composure. Quietly, he levelled his Winchester carbine
and fired two shots. The second round struck a "big
sergeant [who was] sitting on his horse" and who
"threw up his arms and fell . . ." dead. Then, Funston
ran deeper into the glade and again secluded himself and
waited for the enemy, who—to his amusement—feared
to penetrate the forest after him and shortly rode off in
another direction. Funston crept back to the sergeant's
body, examined his fallen foe, and, as he remembered
later, "did not feel any compunction of conscience
whatever for killing him, . . ." Rather, he "looked down
at him just as . . . [he] would have looked at a wolf or a
bear that . . . [he] had killed."

   Sometime later, while he was on the march with
Garcia's command, Funston verified the remaining
dozen victims of his own shooting. He was instructed by
the general to bombard a small, isolated stone mill.
Garcia's column had unexpectedly run upon this enemy
installation and had discovered that it was garrisoned by
only a small force of Spaniards. Funston aimed his
Hotchkiss field piece at one of the two second-story
windows from which the enemy were firing their own
field guns, and he put his second round inside the
stronghold, where it detonated. His third shot passed
through the other window and also exploded inside the
Spaniards' fort. "Curious to note the effect of . . . [his]
two shots," Funston entered the mill after the battle
and found twelve dead Spaniards lying about the two
windows through which his shells had whizzed. Again,
there was no remorse; there was just soldierly detachment about the effects of artillery. Underlying everything, there was the implicit belief of Funston that such
grisly events were just part of the dangerous and adventurous game of war in which all real men took their
chances and uncomplainingly accepted the outcome.[4]

   Yet, though he was greatly incapacitated by his

[4] William H. Sears to Richard J. Oulahan, February 27, 1917, *ibid.*

physical injuries, and though he was satisfied personally by the course of his service for the Cubans, Funston could not easily leave Cuba. He could not simply wander off to the beach and catch the *Dauntless*, or another of her ilk, for a quick cruise home. He was a high-ranking officer who was acting under military regulations, and he faced the necessity of behaving accordingly.

Following the *insurrectos'* capture of the Spanish town of *Guisa* on November 28, 1897, Funston made the first official move toward his return home. He asked that General Garcia grant him a leave so that he could travel to the United States, where he might receive good medical attention and enjoy a complete recuperation. He had been too debilitated to participate in the successful siege of *Guisa*, and he recognized that the artillery unit had acquitted itself well in the operation without him. He therefore thought that the time was ripe for his request. To strengthen his bid, he accompanied his plea to Garcia with his promise to return to duty in Cuba as soon as his health permitted. Garcia, who was kindly by nature and who well knew of Funston's sad physical condition, granted leave at once. The general also allowed similar privileges to James Pennie, who was one of Funston's fellow countrymen. A lieutenant, Pennie was gravely ill with *paludismo*, and he intended to go with Funston to the northern coast, where the pair hoped to contact a filibustering tug.

There was, however, a bureaucratic complication that was connected with Funston's getting full, authoritative permission for a leave. Since he was a lieutenant-colonel, he was, technically, an officer of staff rank under the regulations that the *insurrecto* army followed. As a consequence, Funston had to get the *insurrectos'* civil government, the Cuban republican government that the rebels had proclaimed, to approve Garcia's decision before he could legally depart the island. Funston and

Pennie traveled by horseback to the town of *Aguaro*, in *Camaguey* Province, where the Cuban assembly and other republican authorities were then sitting.

Funston and Pennie presented the passes that Garcia had given them to the officials, and they coupled their parcel of documents with a fulsome appeal to the assembly that Funston composed in Spanish on December 4, 1897. Funston first pointed to Pennie's twenty months of service and then to his own sixteen months of duty. He stated that they were "truly broken in health and also further emaciated by the rigors of the climate." He declared that they had come to Cuba, not for profit, but "only with the desire of helping to see that she [Cuba] was soon free from the despotic Spanish yoke." It was their hope, Funston concluded, that the *insurrecto* army would continue to triumph and that the government would soon have the good fortune to put the country on the way toward strong posperity and complete unity. In short, what Funston meant was that they were sick, had done their duty, still loved the cause, but wanted now to go home only in order to get cured by physicians in the United States.

Surprisingly, the reply to the petition that was made officially by the Secretary of War was negative. The government stated that they saw no "case of imperative necessity" in the situations of Funston and Pennie, and they turned down the pleas of both officers to go to the United States. Perhaps, the civil authorities had heard too many such requests. Perhaps, they had seen too many men who were in as bad physical shape as were Funston and Pennie. Perhaps, the Cubans simply were too hardened by years of war and suffering among their own people to heed the petition of two foreigners. It may have been that there was jealousy of Garcia among the government, and, since they enjoyed the general's blessing, Funston and Pennie became the means by which a few, well-placed, spiteful persons struck at the famous rebel *jefe*.

Whatever the reasons, Funston and Pennie were now in a desperate quandary. They could either accept the civil leaders' decision, return to Garcia, and probably eventually die from lack of good medical care as their health grew progressively worse, or they could violate orders and strike out for the coast in the hope that Garcia's passes would get them berths aboard a filibustering vessel that was returning to the mainland. If they took the latter alternative, they ran the risk of alienating many Cubans and besmirching their records as *insurrecto* soldiers; this would make any claims for back pay that they might make later once Cuba was free useless. Yet, the stark truth remained that if they remained on the island, they probably would die. For a week following their plea's rejection by the government, the pair simply lay out in a field that was near the offices of the Cuban authorities. Weak and ailing, lacking medicine, and even their hammocks, they were hoping that the government would perhaps relent. Finally, out of sheer desperation, Funston and Pennie opted to go for the coast and hope for the best.[5]

[5] A. Prats-Lerma, "La Actuacion del Teniente Coronel Frederick Funston," *Boletin del Ejercito*, Nov.-Dec., 1931, pp. 376-377; Untitled Newspaper Interview, Topeka, Kansas, *Daily Capital*, January 12, 1898, F. Funston Papers, Box 75; there are several other possible explanations for the motivations that might have caused the Cuban civil authorities to turn down Funston's and Pennie's request for medical leave. Perhaps, the Cuban government simply believed that an officer of the rank of lieutenant colonel should not ask to depart while the war still raged. Perhaps, the Cuban authorities acted indirectly for Garcia, who might have discreetly informed the government that Funston's skill was essential to his command. Perhaps, some Cubans disliked Funston—and North American volunteers in general—and believed that their hardships warranted no more consideration than those that were being incurred by native-born *insurrectos*. Anyway, it is certain that Pennie's request was linked by the Cubans with Funston's and suffered the fate of Funston's. The author has been unable to find out whether Pennie was able to leave Cuba alive.

As they rode toward the ocean on December 12, 1897, Funston's horse pulled a few yards ahead of Pennie's and, before many miles, the two were moving "along a dusty road," to the "immediate left [of which] was a very high railroad grade." They were adjacent to the rail line that ran between *Nuevitas* and *Puerto Principe*, and it was an obstruction that they had to cross in order to approach the beach that lay to the North.

Finally, Funston, who was still in the lead, saw that ahead the way "turned sharply to the left" and then ran up and over the tracks. Eager to see what lay on the other side of the rail embankment, Funston "spurred . . . [his] horse forward to a gallop, . . . topped the grade [,] . . . [and] was confronted by a row of Spanish rifles behind it, . . ." Immediately, a gruff Spanish command to identify himself broke the silence and revealed to Funston what he had done. He had blundered upon an outpost of six enemy soldiers, and, depending upon how he reacted in the next few moments, he was either a prisoner or a dead man.

Though he was quite weak from his illnesses and weary from his travelling, Funston was yet mentally acute and as resourceful as always. Quickly, he threw up his hands in an exaggerated movement that warned Pennie and allowed him to ride away to safety. Then, speaking to captors in his best, rapidfire Spanish, he gave a bogus name. Funston ardently claimed that he was a *"presentado,"* an *insurrecto* who was tired of the war and was looking for Spaniards to whom he could surrender honorably. He also alleged that he held valuable information for the Spanish. This ruse probably saved Funston from death on the spot. Yet, he was still in grave danger, for if they had discovered his true identity and rank, information that his pass from Garcia bore, the Spaniards would surely have shot him forth-with. So, continuing to talk, he denounced "the Revolutionists in the most violent terms, . . ." He admitted that he had fought with the rebels, but he proclaimed most emphatically to his half-dozen captors that he now "was sick of . . . [the *insurrectos*] and their methods and was deserting."

This story continued to be Funston's explanation of his presence throughout his captivity by the Spaniards, who finally accepted it as plausible. The tale also gave Funston some vital time during his first few minutes as a prisoner, and he used this interval to destroy his pass, since its contents would have shown him as a liar and meant his execution. While he was giving his initial tirade against the revolution, Funston pulled out his handkerchief that he had wrapped about his pass in order to protect it. As he was damning the insurrection, he swiped the cloth across his face as though he wished to wipe away an accumulation of perspiration. Such a normal and casual movement roused no suspicion among the Spaniards, and it afforded Funston the crucial opportunity to slip the damaging paper pass into his mouth and quickly swallow it. Though the wad of dirty cellulose caused him to suffer an attack of indigestion, Funston's impromptu "meal" enabled him to maintain his facade as a jaded turncoat and hence saved his life.

The Spaniards were convinced by Funston of his sincerity, though they were not willing to trust him completely. The Spanish sentries bound Funston hand and foot, and then they took him to their post at *Las Minas*. Subsequently, other guards conveyed him to *Puerto Principe*, where General Castellanos, who was the Spanish commander of the area, maintained his headquarters. For a second time, Funston told his story. General Castellanos, who this time was his chief listener, finally "convened a special board of inquiry, consisting of six members," who caused the prisoner to spin his tale a third time. This panel was actually a court martial, and legally they could have decreed the death penalty under the aegis of those of Captain-General Weyler's stern policies that yet remained viable. However, the half-dozen officers chose to believe Funston.

Perhaps, it was the lack of evidence to contradict his false name and cover story that convinced the court. Perhaps, Funston's "cooperation" won them over, becuase the emaciated, shabbily-dressed prisoner—whose demeanor and accent undoubtedly did not long allow him to pretend to be a native Cuban—made revelations about the *insurrecto* army and its operations. However, in feigning contrition to save his life, Funston was careful to mix generous amounts of fiction with the facts that he estimated that the Spaniards already knew. He concocted an elaborate yarn that was replete with spurious information, and he fully believed that he had not in reality betrayed his comrades. At any rate, after the first few hours, the Spanish consistently treated their prisoner well throughout his detainment, and they in due course decided that he and his story were authentic. Finally, they even offered him a parole, provided that he would swear an oath never again to aid the rebel cause. Funston agreed and made the affirmation. Afterwards, late in December, 1897, the Spaniards transported him by ship to *Habana,* where he contacted the United States Consul.

Later, when he was describing his interrogation at *Puerto Principe* to Charles Scott, Funston made light of his experiences as a Spanish prisoner. He facetiously declared that he had

> lied to that Court Martial [;] that ought to stultify me forever. It . . . [was] not a handsome [thing] to say that I did, but just after my acquital I borrowed a copy of the statutes of Mesa potanis [sic] and found the following paragraph,:—"lying is bad business, but it is better that a string of

whoppers be told than that a Kansas man should spend many months in a Spanish jail."[6]

Certainly, the venerable Fitzhugh Lee, the ex-Confederate soldier who was a Consul and was now the active representative of United States interests in the colonial island's capital, agreed heartily with Funston that his fellow countrymen should avoid Spanish jails at any price. A staunch and aggressive protector of those North Americans who were residing in Cuba, Fitzhugh Lee had already accumulated much experience in dealing with cases such as that Funston now constituted. In fact, the record of his truculence in defending the rights of United States citizens in Cuba may have been a factor in the court martial's decision to free Funston. Upon his arrival in *Habana* in June, 1896, Lee had begun at once to protest to General Valeriano Weyler about the incommunicado detainment of North Americans. Later, the Spanish had unjustly accused an American-born dentist of rebel activities and jailed him arbitrarily. They had mistreated the dentist while he was being held by them incommunicado, and they had caused his death.

[6] "Brigadier-General Funston," *The World's Work*, May, 1901, p. 697; Charles F. Scott, "Frederick Funston," *The Independent*, April 11, 1901, p. 820; C. S. Gleed, "Romance and Reality," *Cosmopolitan*, July, 1899, p. 328; F. F. Eckdall, "'Fighting' Fred Funston," Speech in *The Kansas State Historical Quarterly*, Spring, 1956, p. 81; "Frederick Funston," *Harper's Weekly*, March 5, 1898, p. 226; Frederick Funston to Charles F. Scott, January 13, 1898, New York City, New York, F. Funston Papers, Box 75; Louis S. Young and Henry D. Northrop, *Life and Heroic Deeds of Admiral Dewey*, pp. 346-347; "Personal Glimpses—'Fighting' Fred Funston," *The Literary Digest*, May 23, 1914, p. 1270; "Persons in the Foreground: The Adventurous Career of Frederick Funston," *Current Opinion*, June, 1914, p. 428; Untitled Newspaper Article, Kansas City, Missouri, *Times*, January 14, 1936, Section D, p. 16, c. 3-4; Untitled Newspaper Article, New York *Times*, April 30, 1899, p. 6, c. 5-6; Untitled Newspaper Article, Topeka, Kansas, *Daily Capital*, March [?], 1898, F. Funston Papers, Box 75; Untitled Newspaper Interview, Topeka, Kansas, *Daily Capital*, January 12, 1898, *ibid.*; William H. Sears to Richard J. Oulahan, February 27, 1917, Lawrence, Kansas, William H. Sears Papers, *Kansas State Historical Society*, Topeka, Kansas.

After this unfortunate incident, Fitzhugh Lee had determined to work in behalf of any of his countrymen who might be imprisoned by the Spaniards on the devastated island to the utmost of his abilities. In consequence, on another occasion, his demands had obtained the freedom of a United States citizen whom the Spaniards had seized, and he had set an important precedent. From that point forward, the Spanish saw to it that Lee habitually received all Americans whom they had captured. Lee's policy was to look after the immediate needs of his released countrymen and then, as quickly as possible, furnish them with the means of a safe return to the United States.[7]

Accordingly, the paroled Funston, once he had arrived in *Habana,* was close to effective help. As soon as the Spaniards let him go, he made his way directly to the office of the United States Consul. Busy at his desk that late December day when Funston entered his chamber, Lee did not at first realize that he had a guest. Then, hearing a noise, he looked up. Lee was immensely startled to behold the form of the bedraggled Kansas *expedicionario* standing before him. The Consul at once concluded that the "disreputable-looking character" that was confronting him was an "assassin," and he reflexively grasped the butt of his ever-present revolver and told his visitor to throw up his hands and identify himself. Funston, who indeed looked the part of a desperado with his long and shaggy hair, untrimmed beard, well-ventilated hat, worn-out shoes, and near nakedness, immediately complied with Lee's demands. It was fortunate that he did not protest and complain, for the Consul declared later that one false move on the part of that scraggly figure who was clad only in a dirty and ragged linen duster would have meant his death.

[7] Fitzhugh Lee, "Cuba and Her Struggle for Freedom," *The Fortnightly Review,* June 1, 1898, pp. 861-862.

Once Funston had convinced Lee of his authenticity and purpose, the atmosphere in the office abruptly changed from tense hostility to congenial sympathy. Lee chuckled, and, motioning to his intruder to take a seat, he admitted to Funston that he had been "a rebel once, too." The Consul commented humorously on Funston's seedy appearance, saying, "but damme [sic] if I was as bad a looking rebel as you are!" At once, Lee began to make arrangements to care for Funston's needs and to get the enfeebled *expedicionario* back to New York on the first available ship. The Consul obtained presentable clothes for Funston and forked over the money to the Ward Line for his passage on a steamer that was bound for the mouth of the Hudson River. Before mid-January, his debilitated charge was safely back in the city that he had left on his furtive transit almost a year and a half previously.[8]

[8] Louis S. Young and Henry D. Northrop, *Life and Heroic Deeds of Admiral Dewey*, p. 347; New York *Times Magazine*, February 25, 1917, pp. 1-2; "Persons in the Foreground: The Adventurous Career of Frederick Funston," *Current Opinion*, June, 1914, p. 428.

# 10

## The Hero of Kansas

Just because he had at last reached the soil of the United States did not mean that Funston forthwith put an end to his Cuban trials. When he disembarked in New York harbor on January 10, 1898, in the midst of a heavy snow storm, he possessed only the "ice cream suit" of white ducking that Lee had bought for him in *Habana*, and carried only $6.00 in his pockets. While it was true that he was something of a celebrity, and while he held several newspaper interviews during his first few days back in New York City, Funston personally was in dire straits. He sorely needed immediate and extensive medical treatment. Consequently, material assets and notoriety were the least of his concerns.

So grave had been his physical rigors in Cuba that he now constituted a veritable, walking medical encyclopedia of tropical ailments and battle wounds. The injuries in his left arm and lungs had healed reasonably well, but their effects had contributed to his general, rundown condition. He was yet lame in his left leg. This latter difficulty was caused ultimately by the abcess that festered deep inside his left hip. This was an infected mass that stubbornly refused to heal and remained a serious medical problem for Funston for months to come.

Moreover, malaria had graced the emaciated frame of Funston, who now weighed less than 100 pounds, with a pale, patina of fevered nervousness. Some of those who saw Funston upon his return, in fact, believed that he had "aged ten years" during his seventeen-month tour in Cuba. Funston himself admitted that he "certainly . . . [felt] pretty old" and that he was "in a bad fix physically." He wisely concluded that his only recourse was to delay his departure for Kansas "for three weeks or a month" in order "to go into a hospital and be cut into small slices [,] and then lie in bed until . . . [he grew] together again."

Surprisingly, in view of his depleted physical condition, Funston responded well and rapidly to his hospitalization. All told, he remained "stretched out on . . . [his] back" for three weeks. He lay in an institution that was on New York City's 32nd Street, and "a large rude surgeon" who was a member of the hospital's staff gave him close attendance and applied the knife to his troublesome hip wound. In spite of this surgery, Funston regained ten of his lost pounds during the first two weeks of his convalescence. The rest and medicine also quickly dispelled "that hideous yellow of the jungle fever" from his skin color. As a result, although he was not in possession of his full health until early April, Funston soon was able to take interest in things other than his recuperation.

Aside from corresponding with his Kansas friends to express his joy at his pending homecoming, the rapidly mending former-*expedicionario* showed his returning vigor in another way. Funston hit at some of the exaggerated accounts of his physical condition that had been carried by the press. He angrily lashed out at a score of eastern newspaper reporters who had seen him on the day of his arrival and who had made him out in their articles as a man who was unquestionably "crippled for life." Funston thought that these newsmen were just sensationalists; they had written their pieces solely with the aim of depicting him as a man who was pleading for public sympathy. Specifically, Funston moved to disabuse those in Kansas who might have accepted this erroneous image of himself. He wrote to Charles E. Scott that, within a month, he would be able to outrun every one of those "lying reporters" who had styled him a broken man. He related to Scott that these newspapermen had interviewed him on a day on which his infected hip had been paining him very badly. He believed that these over-eager men of the press, in struggling to attract readers, had let their proclivity for sensationalism run away with them, even though he had expressly "told them . . . [that his] injury was only temporary." Frederick Funston, whose strength was rapidly returning, was not about to allow careless, news-hungry journalists to give him a wrongful appearance, and he was recuperated enough to be fully angry over the episode. He was anything but a physically-ruined mendicant who was pathetically and desperately appealing for public sympathy and aid.[1]

Actually, the convalesing veteran had more reason than that of the distorted story of his hip wound to be

---

[1] A. Prats-Lerma, "La Actuacion del Teniente Coronel Frederick Funston," *Boletin del Ejercito*, Nov.-Dec., 1931, p. 377; "Brigadier-General Funston," *World's Work*, May, 1901, p. 697; C. S. Gleed, "Romance and Reality," *Cosmopolitan*, July, 1899, p. 327; Charles F. Scott, "Frederick Funston," *The Independent*, April 11, 1901, p. 820; Frederick Funston to Charles F. Scott, January 13, 1898, New York City, New York, F. Funston Papers, Box 75 (Reprinted in Iola, Kansas, *Daily Register*, January 19, 1898, and in Topeka, Kansas, *Daily Capital*, January 20, 1898); Frederick Funston to Charles F. Scott, January 18, 1898, New York City, New York; and Frederick Funston to Charles F. Scott, January 24, 1898, New York City, New York; both of these letters come from F. Funston Papers, Box 75; Frederick Funston to Frank Webster, January 14, 1898, New York City, New York (Reprinted in Topeka, Kansas, *Daily Capital*, January 19, 1898), F. Funston Papers, Box 75; New York *Times*, April 30, 1898, p. 6, c. 5-6; "Personal Glimpses—He Snared Aguinaldo," *The Literary Digest*, March 10, 1917, p. 641; Uncited and Undated Newspaper Feature Article, Entitled "Funstoniana—'F. F., General Career' ", F. Funston Papers, Box 75; William Allen White, "Gen. Frederick Funston," *Harper's Weekly*, May 20, 1899, p. 496; in his *Memories of Two Wars*, p. 142, Funston, with characteristic self-deprecation, merely stated that he was "temporarily broken in health" when he returned to the United States from Cuba in 1898.

picqued at the newsmen of the New York City area. In answering the reporters' questions during an interview on January 10, Funston had remarked about the back salary that was due him from the Cubans because of his several months' service as an *insurrecto* artillery officer. In his comments, he based his calculations of pay expectations on the rate of pay per month in American gold dollars, and he reckoned that he would receive "about $4,000"—once the Cubans had won their independence. Funston never took in most of this handsome sum, partly because he was in the Philippines when the *insurrectos* finally settled accounts with their *expedicionarios*. However, Funston's even mentioning his sizeable accrued compensation created some difficulties for him in early 1898. Funston's revelation motivated one youthful newspaper scribe who was present at the interview to rush directly off to see Tomas Estrada Palma, who was yet the *junta's* leader in New York City.

This cub journalist, who, in ex-newspaperman Funston's eyes, was just "a wild eyed young ass of a reporter," garbled the colonel's name to "Furston" when he talked to Palma. Consequently, Palma did not recognize that the appellation referred to Funston. Moreover, Palma concluded that the name "Furston" had nothing to do with any North American who had ever served Cuba, and hence the man who bore it deserved no payment whatsoever. Subsequently, the blundering reporter made matters even worse. He got his subject's name straight when he wrote his article, but he still telegraphed his "scoop" all over the United States to the effect that the Cuban *junta* did not know and did not claim "Frederick Funston"!

Understandably, Funston was much angered by the incident, and he determined to straighten out matters right away. He persuaded Charles Scott to prevail upon his father, erstwhile-Congressman Funston, to telegraph a protest about the newspaper account to the *junta*. In addition, as soon as his health permitted, he himself called on the Cuban revolutionary council. Finally, these moves cleared up the confusion, and the New York *insurrectos* "proceded to do the right thing by . . . [Funston] ," who, in due course, received a small portion of his service pay. He also got an assurance that the rebels would foot the costs of his New York City medical care.[2]

Funston, who was now just a demobilized *insurrecto* without money in New York City, appreciated the *junta's* limited financial help, but he was still virtually penniless when he finally arrived at his home near Iola early in February, 1898. Several alternatives appeared feasible to Funston at this juncture, when it came to the matter of his making money. For one thing, he might have borrowed sums from his friends to tide him over until he got on his feet financially. Charles Scott generously offered him a loan, but Funston refused it by commenting that he had "a horror of being in debt even to . . . [his] most intimate friends. . ." Besides, he told Scott that he was "a little in debt already, but not much, . . ." A second avenue that might have led to monetary gain for Funston lay in the area of writing. This endeavor was one in which Funston had experienced modest success, and the attraction of earning

[2] A. Prats-Lerma, *ibid.*, p. 362; Frederick Funston to Charles F. Scott, January 18, 1898, *ibid.*; Frederick Funston to E. H. Funston, March 5, 1897, In Camp, Headquarters, Department of *Oriente*, Cuba, F. Funston Papers, Box 75; Uncited and Untitled Newspaper Article, "From a Kansas paper [sic] of January 11, 1898," F. Funston Papers, Box 75; Untitled Newspaper Interview, Topeka, Kansas, *Daily Capital*, January 12, 1898, F. Funston Papers, Box 75; while it seems probable that the New York Cuban *junta* paid Funston's hospital bill, Funston—as far as the author can determine—made no express comment to this effect. For certain, he received medical care, and he needed money when he reached Kansas. Funston's lecturing for fees in Kansas might not have meant necessarily that he owed the New York hospital and its doctors, but, rather, it might have indicated that he simply lacked any financial resources and wanted to accrue some.

money by his pen had helped draw his interest to Cuba originally. Before he left New York City for Kansas, he had received indications from the editors of both *Harper's* and *Scribner's* magazines that they were interested in running a series of his Cuban articles that related his experiences as an *insurrecto*.

Before he could sell accounts of his adventures, Funston had first to take time out to collect his thoughts, and then he had to sit down and compose his narratives. It was several years before the press of events allowed Funston the time that was necessary to do this writing. The coming of the Spanish War in April, 1898, and Funston's United States military service that began with that conflict in part explained the tardy appearance of the greater part of the writing that he did about his Cuban adventures.

Also, there was something that acted as an immediate hindrance to any serious authorship by Funston during these early weeks of 1898. Feeling himself financially pinched, Funston reluctantly decided to capitalize on his state-wide fame in Kansas. He determined to give a series of public lectures that dealt with his experiences as an *expedicionario* in Cuba. While the speaking circuit was more than a little distasteful to him, Funston believed that his lecturing to the Kansas public was the best way for him to raise a sizeable amount of money in a hurry. He was an experienced professional lecturer, because he had capitalized on his local fame as an Arctic explorer after his second Alaskan adventure and toured Kansas to raise capital for his ill-fated, Mexican coffee scheme. Even before he had left his New York City hospital bed, he received queries from the Chautauqua societies of both Kansas City, Missouri, and Ottawa, Kansas, about the possibility of his giving lectures to their membership. And, Funston was cognizant of the fact that Scott's publishing some of his letters in the Iola *Daily Register* had helped to create interest in his

life as an *insurrecto*. Funston's name was now one that
was familiar to people who lived all across the Jayhawk
state.[3]

Consequently, Funston spent much of his time between early February and mid-April, 1898, giving public
talks for fees at various towns of his home state. He
went at the project in a business-like manner and hired
as his manager J. A. Young, an experienced sponsor of
speaking tours who worked out of Kansas City, Missouri. Funston and Young entered into a contract that
was to run from February 16 to June 1. They agreed on
a sliding scale for dividing the profits and worked out
the various necessary arrangements to their mutual satisfaction.

So it was that Funston made the rounds of the
Kansas lecture platforms in early 1898. He charged
admissions of 35¢, or thereabouts, per person, and he
happily found that, while the size of his audiences
varied greatly, his remarks were always warmly received
by his listeners. He usually sent around a printed handbill in advance of his appearances in order to build up
interest in his talks among any potential local sponsors.

One of these circulars—probably a typical member
of its genre—bore the title, "On the Inside of the Cuban
Revolution." The sheet carried a head-and-shoulders
photograph of a bearded Funston. He was wearing his
panama hat and was clad in a white duck shirt that was
partly covered by his lieutenant-colonel's sash with its
two gold stars of rank. This badge of status ran diagonal-
ly across Funston's chest from his right shoulder to his
waist. The handbill proclaimed that anyone who heard
the speaker would learn, "The Real Facts [*sic*] about

---

[3] Frederick Funston to Charles F. Scott, January 18, 1898, *ibid.*; Frederick
Funston to Charles F. Scott, January 24, 1898, New York City, New York,
F. Funston Papers, Box 75; Topeka, Kansas, *Daily Capital*, February 20,
1917, p. 1, c. 5.

the struggle for independence told by one who Marched and Fought in the Armies of Gomez and Garcia." There followed a synopsis of Funston's Cuban service and a promise that "in his lecture Col. Funston" would describe "graphically . . . a number of the more important battles, . . ." He would also relate "many of the incidents of the camp and march, and . . . his experience in prison and trial by court martial."

Apparently, such printed advertising was effective in Kansas during 1898, because Funston's lecture tour was a successful venture. Everywhere in Kansas, he seemed to please audiences with his timely remarks on Cuba, the island that was daily before the public in the press. Nowhere did he score a bigger success than in Topeka, the state's capital city, where he spoke early in March. Arriving on the noon train, Funston found himself confronted by a string of carriages that were occupied by a delegation of some of the city's leading citizens. The mayor of Topeka extended an official welcome to Funston and personally conducted him to his hotel room by means of a special carriage that was decorated with a Cuban flag. Throughout the afternoon, old friends and members of the capital city's press corps called to talk with Funston and obtain his own views on Spanish-American relations. This subject was now especially interesting to Kansans, since the recent, mysterious destruction of the U.S.S. *Maine* in *Habana* harbor had greatly raised tension between Spain and the United States. Funston, however, declined to comment extensively on the Cuban situation at *Habana,* since he had been there only briefly. Yet, he did venture an opinion in regard to the Spaniards at *Habana* and their connections with the *Maine* disaster. It was his feeling that, since there were probably "submarine mines" in *Habana* harbor, "the *Maine* was [accidentally] blown up . . ." Funston did not think that "the Spanish officials were the authors of the tragedy."

That night at 8 P.M., Funston spoke to an impressive audience that was seated amidst imposing arrangements. Members of the local Elks' lodge, who were the colonel's sponsors here, acted as ushers. On the stage of the auditorium, an orchestra played. A huge map of Cuba ran across the rear of the platform and served as a background. Following his flattering introduction by the Elks' president, Funston spoke, abiding by the same outline that he had by now well developed. He related the background of "the Ten Years' War," the subsequent failure of promised Spanish reforms, the beginnings and the course of the '95 rebellion, and then a description of his own adventures. He told of his recruitment, transit, battle experiences, and personal impressions of people and places. He even included his days as a prisoner of the Spanish, for whom, to the surprise of Kansans, he had some kind words. Funston declared that the Spanish had treated him well. He said Spaniards were generally not guilty of any savagery like that committed by their loyalist allies, the Cuban *guerrilleros*. Funston proclaimed that he was strongly in favor of United States intervention in the war, for neither side would ever quit fighting otherwise, and Cuban society and wealth would never recover from the devastation of the rebellion, if the war continued much longer.

Usually, as his Topeka address indicated, Funston was an engrossing speaker on his tour. He generally left his audience with the feeling that they had received their money's worth. After he had spoken at the First Presbyterian Church at Emporia, the local press employed the laudatory adjectives "most entertaining," "unstudied," "unassuming," and "graceful" to describe the former-*insurrecto's* two-hour long presentation. The Emporia newspaper also pointed out that the audience had frequently interrupted Funston's comments with outbursts of heavy applause. Even when the large crowd that he had anticipated failed to materialize, Funston came across with his usual interesting story to the "small, but pleased audience." Such was the case at Turner Hall in Marysville, Kansas, on April 13, 1898. In this instance, Funston, who was now "lecturing every other day," found that the Marysville high school alumni association, his local sponsors, had not pushed the advance sale of tickets. The result of the slack effort was that the Marysville group was able to pay Funston only $16.00 of the $75.00 that Funston and the local backers had agreed would be the fee for the speech. Yet, one Marysville man remembered that Funston "was perfectly satisfied under the circumstances." Probably, Funston assumed—and correctly so—that his partner Young could recover the balance of the fee later.

Funston profited financially at the speaker's rostrum by relating his adventures as an *insurrecto*. In spite of his inability to get his full back pay from the Cuban republicans, Funston was able to capitalize on his Cuban service. Through his lectures, he was able to accumulate a sum of money during the early spring of 1898 and make his soldiering pay him something in a monetary way after all.[4]

Aside from giving these remunerative lectures, Funston spent his time renewing old acquaintances and visiting family. As he carried on his tour and his pleasurable social contacts, his strength slowly returned, and his body mended, and as his physical condition bettered, he

[4] Copy of Contract between Frederick Funston and J. A. Young, dated February 16, 1898, F. Funston Papers, Box 76; Doctor Charles A. Arand to *The Kansas State Historical Society*, September 25, 1936, Sault Ste. Marie, Michigan (Enclosures, including handbills, one a draft in Funston's own hand advertising his lecture at Marysville, Kansas, and one a general printed advertisement, telling interested sponsors to contact J. A. Young), *The Kansas State Historical Society*, Topeka, Kansas; Untitled Newspaper Article, Emporia, Kansas, *Gazette*, "Feb. or March of 1898 [sic]," F. Funston Papers, Box 75.

reveled in being back home and seeing those who were closest to him. To his kin, his college chums, and other Kansas intimates, he accorded the privilege of hearing at first-hand the "un-edited," humorous accounts of his Cuban experiences. During these private exchanges, he usually made himself appear as a bumbling adventurer who only saw the funny side of war. His comrades, however, were always serious and effective men who were brave and outstanding as well.

Funston enjoyed an especially close relationship with William Allen White, the active and intelligent journalist of Emporia. When he talked with White, he told of the past in Cuba, but he also considered the feasibility of his capitalizing on his war fame in a practical way aside from lecturing and going into Republican politics. This electioneering business, however, was really against his grain. White had little difficulty in persuading Funston to let the Republican machinery of Kansas continue their merry way without his services.[5]

Meanwhile, on the far side of the Gulf of Mexico, the Cuban insurrection was still raging. Amidst the rumors and gossip of this continuing war, Funston's reputation was being assailed by some *insurrectos* who had been greatly angered by his departure the preceding December. Some of his old comrades-in-arms took exception to the manner in which Funston had carried out his safe exit from the bitter struggle. These men remembered that those Cubans who were in the rebel army remained soldiers until either death, or complete disability, or victory demobilized them. Also, they recalled that, while, in theory, foreign volunteers had the privilege of quitting any time that they so desired, the situation, in fact, for *expedicionarios* was different. Before they left Cuba, *expedicionarios* first were supposed

[5] William Allen White, *Autobiography*, p. 306.

to obtain official permission for their absences from the Cuban Republic's civil authorities.[6]

While a number of Funston's rebel colleagues stood by him in this matter, many others—perhaps because Funston held the high rank of lieutenant colonel—condemned him for his Spanish-aided departure from Cuba. These detractors were influential enough to keep a damning story against Funston alive for several years. The thrust of this allegation was that Funston, despite the promotions and honors that the rebels had accorded him, left the Cuban cause dishonorably and at a critical moment. Possibly, what was resented by these critics, who forgot Funston's distinguished service and severe suffering, was that Funston had claimed a false identity and subsequently given his amended information about the rebel forces to his Spanish captors in order to save his life. The exact reason was obscure, but the existence of an enmity toward Funston as late as the fall of 1906 was a fact. This hostility later proved unfortunate for the Kansas soldier during the second Cuban intervention of 1906. At that point, Funston, who was well along in his career as a general officer in the regular army of the United States, needed all the Cuban goodwill that he could muster.[7]

[6] Emory W. Fenn, "Ten Months with the Cuban Insurgents," *Century*, June, 1898, p. 307; Frederick Funston, "A Defeat and a Victory," *Scribner's*, December, 1910, p. 754. The Spanish captured Emory in January, 1898, as he was trying to leave Cuba. When they found out he was telling the truth about his destination—the United States on family business—and that he was not on a mission for the rebels, they turned him over to Fitzhugh Lee for transportation to the United States. They did this in spite of the fact that he was carrying letters from members of Garcia's staff to their friends in the United States.

[7] Major General Leonard Wood to Captain Frank R. McCoy, September 24, 1906, Headquarters, Philippines Division, Manila, Luzon, Philippine Islands, Frank R. McCoy Papers, Box No. 10, Folder "1-1906"; Captain Frank R. McCoy to Major General Leonard Wood, November 16, 1906, *Habana*, Cuba, Frank R. McCoy Papers, Box No. 14, Folder "Letters 1914-1917", Mss. Division, Library of Congress, Washington, D.C.; Major

The animosity that these Cubans felt toward Funston in the spring of 1898 and afterwards was miniscule in comparison with the bitterness that was being spawned in Cuba by the continuing warfare between the Spanish and the island's republicans. In spite of General Blanco's reversal of the policies of the departed Weyler, and in spite of his offering the Cubans political autonomy within the Spanish empire in late November, 1897, there was very little tranquility on the ravaged island. The fighting went on without any real pause and lapsed over into 1898. Thousands of Cubans were starving; months of bloodletting and looting had left scores of personal *vendettas* unsettled; too many islanders were used to living by plundering and pillaging; and, in addition, the rebel leaders despised the scheme for autonomy and claimed that it gave Madrid too much power over the island legislature's upper chamber, the island's courts, and the island's budget.

As determined as ever to achieve complete independence, Gomez and the other revolutionary leaders terrorized the friends of autonomy. They killed any autonomists whom they caught. In reality, they set out to make Cuba such a scene of unending misery that either Spain would capitulate or the United States would have no choice except to intervene and establish complete and immediate Cuban independence. With the help of the publication of the infamous "De Lôme Letter" of February 9, 1898, and the sensational sinking of the *U.S.S. Maine* in *Habana* harbor on February 16, 1898, they succeeded only too well.

Though events were to deny him a chance to know personally the nature of this Spanish-American conflict

General Leonard Wood to Alexander Gonzales, November 18, 1906, Headquarters, Philippines Division, Manila, Luzon, Philippine Islands, Leonard Wood Papers, General Correspondence, 1906, Box 37, Mss. Division, the Library of Congress, Washington, D.C.

in Cuba, Funston was thrust into the national limelight by the war with Spain. He was the highest-ranking among a handful of "native Americans" who had actually served with the patriot armies in Cuba, because, in spite of the implications of the newspapers, very few North Americans had enlisted in "the cause of liberty." In consequence, he understood intimately—perhaps better than any of his countrymen—the true character of the Spanish-Cuban struggle. During his service in Cuba and, as well, in later years, when he was a professional soldier with greater combat experience, Funston evaluated carefully his months of campaigning as an *insurrecto* against the troops of Weyler and Blanco.

Funston thought that the Cuban *insurrectos*, though they were badly lacking in the forms of traditional military drill, followed "the strictest discipline." He estimated that their civil government worked well everywhere it operated. Moreover, he believed that the Cuban *insurrectos* made excellent scouts and that they possessed fine mobility for organized units of soldiers. Too, he admired the thorough way in which an army that was in nature essentially guerrilla, though it was definitely not an aggregation of bandits as Spain had always alleged, kept full and accurate records. He concluded that the *insurrectos'* history of scores of encounters that stretched over many months and the *insurrectos'* approximately 8,600 deaths from wounds and disease out of an army of only 54,000 strongly indicated the bravery of the Cuban rebels. He had no doubt that the men of Gomez and Garcia were indeed ardent in the cause of independence for their "beautiful and fertile country. . ."

Funston was also mindful of another significant factor of the island war. He knew that the Cubans were outmanned by the Spaniards at a ratio of five to one. Yet, he noted that the *insurrectos* did manage through their efforts to control the interior of Cuba that lay outside of the major towns. In his estimation, it was only a chronic shortage of artillery shells that kept the Cubans from taking more of the large towns from the Spaniards. On a personal and sentimental level, he warmly recalled that the *insurrectos* always were kind to North American *expedicionarios*, no matter what the situation, and he harbored a genuine affection for Cubans in general.

Funston did find some military shortcomings about the *insurrectos*. He faulted his Cuban comrades for their failure to follow up their successes with quick pursuits as well as their proclivity to waste their ammunition. Their lack of care for their equipment and their absence of concern about proper field sanitation verged on appalling Funston. Also the mercurial temperaments of his Cuban comrades had unnerved Funston, because this psychological factor sometimes made the *insurrectos'* conduct unpredictable in tight situations.

Funston also did some evaluating of the Spanish soldiers against whom he had fought on so many occasions. He estimated that the ordinary troopers among the Spaniards usually were brave, long-suffering, and, really, humane fellows who had little heart in the war. Fortunately for the Cubans, these *soldados* habitually became overly excited in combat, and they always aimed their Mauser rifles too high for effective marksmanship. However, they were wonderful executors of the bayonet charge, and this was a Spanish tactic that always enjoyed success and swept the *insurrectos* from the field.

Funston thought well of the Spanish officers whom he had met. Sporting and courteous, these gentlemen did not seem at all villainous to Funston. However, the Kansas fighter strongly criticized the battlefield deployments of the Spaniards' troop commanders. He adamantly maintained that the Spanish officers' preference for fighting their men in close order formations rather than in extended, open ones hurt the Spanish army in Cuba considerably. He thought that this mistake of the Spanish leadership went a long way in explaining the heavy Spanish casualty rate. Funston concluded that the Spanish command's thinking at the upper levels was also of a poor quality. To him, the overall strategy for the island's garrison was poorly conceived by the top officers who uselessly tied up thousands of men in stationary posts that dotted the landscape all across Cuba. Moreover, he thought that Spanish officers were too much addicted to slow and cautious troop movements. Whenever they undertook a military march, the Spanish commanders set the pace of their units too slowly, because they always made up their columns with heavily burdened infantrymen and cumbersome unnecessary transport. These dense, snake-like formations were road bound and crept along at snail's pace. Indeed, these Spanish columns were choice targets for attack by the more rapidly-marching, lightly-encumbered rebels, and generally, because of their mobility, the *insurrectos* held the initiative in the fighting.

Funston declared that he thought that a proper Spanish strategy would have set down altogether different rules to guide the Spanish troops. It would have called for the establishment of a few strong bases on the coast, and then it would have sent highly mobile units fanning out into the interior to press the *insurrectos* hard and persistently and force them to capitulate. He thought that a corps of only 50,000 mounted troops could have carried out this strategy effectively. Funston did, however, credit the Spaniards for one aspect of their Cuban planning, their *"reconcentrados"* policy. He believed that this centralizing of control over the Cuban population could have crushed the insurrection, had the Spanish possessed the resources, determination, and, as well, the unity at home to permit them to enforce the plan as rigorously all over the island as they did in some districts.

In the final analysis, Funston looked upon the insurrection as a military draw, a stalemate that could be broken only by United States intervention. While Spain dominated western Cuba, the rebels ruled the extreme East. The middle section of the island remained an area where the antagonists hotly contested one another for control. Funston's estimations and evaluations probably were correct, but whether Spanish use of Funston's strategy would have ended the rebellion in a victory for Spain can only be a matter of speculation. Nevertheless, it was obvious that the Cuban war did teach Funston to think like a soldier.[8]

Certainly, many of the colonel's friends in Kansas during the spring of 1898 would have argued that he *was* in fact now a soldier. Given his months of arduous duty, his three wounds, and his battlefield promotions, Funston was undoubtedly considered by most Kansans to be a real war hero. He was one of a handful of Americans who possessed varied battle experience against the Spanish, those detested, obnoxious, backward monarchists who were, according to the popular view in the spring of 1898, trying to stop the spread of republican democracy and progress in the Western Hemisphere. He also held recent, first-hand knowledge of men and events in Cuba, where he had participated in some of the bloodiest fighting of the insurrection. Without question, Frederick Funston was a veteran, and his

[8] Frederick Funston, "A Defeat and A Victory," *Scribner's Magazine*, December, 1910, p. 754; Frederick Funston to E. H. Funston, March 5, 1897, In Camp, Headquarters, Department of *Oriente*, Cuba, F. Funston Papers, Box 75; Frederick Funston to Ella Funston, May 10, 1897, In Camp, Headquarters, Department of *Oriente*, Cuba, F. Funston Papers, Box 75; Frederick Funston to Frank Webster, April 10, 1897, In Camp, Headquarters, Department of *Oriente*, near *Holguin*, Cuba (Reprinted in Newspaper), F. Funston Papers, Box 75; Henry Houghton Beck, *Cuba's Fight for Freedom and the War with Spain*, pp. 291-293 and 296-303; Untitled Newspaper Interview, Topeka, Kansas, *Daily Capital*, January 12, 1898, F. Funston Papers, Box 75; Walter Millis, *The Martial Spirit*, pp. 75-76 and 91.

ilk would be in demand should his country suddenly need active and aggressive soldiers who knew the art of modern war. In reality, the Cuban insurrection was the event that turned Funston to soldiering and found for him a career that he could pursue.

In other ways, too, the island war was a signal event in Funston's life. On a personal plane, he developed a warmer appreciation for the ties of family and friendship because of the suffering and deprivation that he witnessed and experienced in Cuba. After his return from this war, he had less use than ever for the "pomp and circumstance" of formal society. To Funston, after the spring of 1898, the demands of living were more clear-cut than ever before. Life was real, pressing, and earnest, and one should not waste it on meaningless, unsatisfying employments or endeavors; time spent with real friends and family was priceless, and there was no point in worrying with those who were not within the precious circle of these relationships.

The war in Cuba also convinced Funston of something else. The United States had a definite, positive role to play in the affairs of the former Spanish colony. He saw this role as that of intervention in order to end the human agonies on the island. Funston believed that the Cuban people, for whom he maintained a life-long friendship and a great admiration, were quite capable of self-government and of building a prosperous, law-abiding society. Yet, to his mind, only the interposition of the might of the United States between *insurrectos* and Spaniards could halt the war and save the Cuban potential for a stable, productive country. Here was the genesis of the concept in Funston's own thinking that his country might also have a "mission" in behalf of stability and "civilization" in less-advanced places. Here was the factor that allowed Funston later to accept a heavier role for his country in the Philippines, whose Oriental populace he found far less capable in matters of self-rule and social and economic progress than he had the populace of his beloved Cuba.

The Cuban Insurrection of 1895-1898, in the long view, gave Frederick Funston his career as a professional soldier. It likewise underscored his beliefs in simple, open, and warm relationships with family and friends as the real bedrock of human existence. And, the year-and-a-half with the cause of the *insurrectos*, fighting as a *guerrillero* in behalf of Cuba's independence from Spain, created in the tough little man from Kansas an unshakeable belief that his country had definite, positive responsibility abroad.

# BIBLIOGRAPHY

## MANUSCRIPTS

*Kansas State Historical Society, Topeka, Kansas.* Charles A. Arand Papers. Frederick Funston Papers. William Henry Sears Papers.

*Manuscripts Division, The Library of Congress, Washington, D.C.* Frank R. McCoy Papers. James W. Wadsworth, Jr., Papers. John J. Pershing Papers. Leonard Wood Papers.

*National Archives and Records Service, The Department of the Interior, Washington, D.C.* Adjutant General's Office 142866. *Documents File Index,* "Funston, Letters, Received" (1898-1917).

## DISSERTATION

Crouch, Thomas W. *The Making of A Soldier: The Career of Frederick Funston, 1865-1902.* The University of Texas (Austin), 1969.

## ARTICLES

"Brigadier-General Funston," *The World's Work* (May, 1901), pp. 678, 696-698.

Crouch, Thomas W. "Frederick Funston In Alaska, 1892-1894: Botany Above the Forty-Ninth Parallel," *Journal of the West,* Volume X, Number 2, April, 1971, pp. 273-306.

_____. "The Funston-Gambrell Dispute: An Episode in Military-Civilian Relations," *Military History of Texas and the Southwest,* Volume IX, Number 2, Spring, 1972, pp. 79-105.

Eckdall, Frank F. " 'Fighting' Fred Funston of Kansas," *The Kansas Historical Quarterly* (Spring, 1956), pp. 78-86. (A

Speech Delivered by Frank F. Eckdall at the Annual Meeting of The Kansas State Historical Society, October 18, 1955, at Topeka, Kansas.)

Fenn, Emory W. "Ten Months With the Cuban Insurgents," *The Century Illustrated Monthly Magazine* (June, 1898), pp. 302-307.

"Frederick Funston," *Harper's Weekly* (March 5, 1898), p. 226.

Funston, Frederick. "A Defeat And A Victory," *Scribner's Magazine* (December, 1910), pp. 735-755.

_____. "Cascorra, The First Cuban Siege," *Scribner's Magazine* (October, 1910), pp. 385-401.

_____. "Desmayo, The Cuban Balaklava," *Harper's Weekly* (March 5, 1898), pp. 225-226.

_____. "The Fall of Guaimaro," *Scribner's Magazine* (November, 1910), pp. 579-595.

_____. "To Cuba As A Filibuster," *Scribner's Magazine* (September, 1910), pp. 305-318.

Gleed, C. S. "Romance and Reality In A Single Life: General Frederick Funston," *Cosmopolitan* (July, 1899), pp. 321-326, 330-331.

Lee, Fitzhugh. "Cuba And Her Struggle For Freedom," *The Fortnightly Review* (June 1, 1898), pp. 854-866.

"Personal Glimpses—'Fightin' Fred' Funston," *The Literary Digest* (May 23, 1914), pp. 1269-1271, 1278-1279.

"Personal Glimpses—He Snared Aguinaldo," *The Literary Digest* (March 10, 1917), pp. 638, 641, 644-645.

Prats—Lerma, Armando. "La Actuacion del Teniente Coronel Frederick Funston (Norte-Americano) en la Guerra de Independencia de 1895-1898," *Bolentin del Ejercito*, Noviembre y Deciembre, 1931, pp. 361-364, 377.

Proctor, Samuel. "Filibustering Aboard *The Three Friends*," *Mid-America, An Historical Review* (April, 1956), pp. 84-100.

Rickenbach, Richard V. "Filibustering With the *Dauntless*," *The Florida Historical Quarterly* (April, 1950), pp. 231-253.

Scott, Charles F. "Frederick Funston," *The Independent* (April 11, 1901), pp. 817-821.

White, William Allen. "Gen. Frederick Funston," *Harper's Weekly* (May 20, 1899), p. 496.

## BOOKS

Batchelor, John, and Hogg, Ian. *Artillery*. New York, New York: Charles Scribner's Sons, 1972.

Beck, Henry Houghton. *Cuba's Fight For Freedom and the War with Spain*. Philadelphia, Pennsylvania: Globe Bible Publishing Company, 1898.

Davis, Richard Harding. *Cuba In War Time*. New York City, New York: R. H. Russell, 1898.

Foner, Philip S. *The Spanish-Cuban-American War and the Birth of American Imperialism*, Volume I, 1895-1898, Volume II, 1898-1902. New York, New York: Monthly Review Press, 1972.

Funston, Frederick. *Memories of Two Wars: Cuban and Philippine Experiences*. New York City, New York: Charles Scribner's Sons, 1911.

Grenville, John A. S., and Young, George Berkeley. *Politics, Strategy, and American Diplomacy: Studies in Foreign Policy, 1873-1917*. New Haven, Connecticut: Yale University Press, 1966.

Healy, David F. *The United States in Cuba, 1898-1902: Generals, Politicians, and the Search for Policy*. Madison, Wisconsin: The University of Wisconsin Press, 1963.

Millis, Walter. *The Martial Spirit*. Cambridge, Massachusetts: The Riverside Press, 1931.

Morgan, Howard Wayne. *William McKinley and His America*. Syracuse, New York: Syracuse University Press, 1963.

White, William Allen. *The Autobiography of William Allen White*. New York City, New York: The MacMillan Company, 1946.

Young, Louis S., and Northrop, Henry D. *Life and Heroic Deeds of Admiral Dewey, Including Battles in the Philippines*. Philadelphia, Pennsylvania: World Bible House, 1899.

## NEWSPAPERS

Kansas City, Missouri, *Journal*, February 25, 1917.
Kansas City, Missouri, *Times*, January 14, 1936.
New York *Times*, April 30, 1899, and February 25, 1917.
Topeka, Kansas, *Daily Capital*, February 20, 1917.

# INDEX

United States for medical care, 123–128; Cuban civil government refuses Frederick Funston's request for medical furlough, 128–130; attempts to get to coast in order to catch ship for the United States, 130–131; is captured, tried, but paroled by Spaniards, 131–133; is aided by United States Consul at *Habana* to return to New York City, 133–136; hospitalized upon arrival in New York City, 137–138; quarrels with the press, 138–140; receives offers to write articles on Cuba, 140–141; decides to give lectures in Kansas about Cuba in order to raise money for his debts and expenses, 141–143; nature of lectures, Funston's views on Cuban situation, and Funston's reunion with family and friends, 143–147; animosity in Cuba toward Frederick Funston, 147–148; Frederick Funston's critique of military operations and policies of the combatants in the Cuban Insurrection, 1895–1898, 149–153; impact of service as an *expedicionario* upon Frederick Funston, 153–155.

Garcia, Calixto, 45; 46; assists Maximo Gomez in laying siege to *Guaimaro*, 70–81;

87; 88; 89; 93; besieges *Jiguani* without success, 94–101; resumes guerrilla operations, 101–102; fights Spaniards at Bay of *Banes*, 102–104; successful in siege of *Victoria de Las Tunas*, 109–120; promotes Frederick Funston to rank of lieutenant colonel, 120; fulfills *expedicionarios'* request to raise black artillery sergeant to lieutenant's rank, 120–121; 123; 127–128.

Garcia, Carlos, 73; 117.
Gleed, Charles S., 15; 16; 26.
Gleed, J. Willis, 26.
Gomez, Maximo, 37; strategy and tactics in Cuban Insurrection, 39–47; welcomes Funston to Cuba, 49–51; directs siege of *Cascorra*, 55–62; presses Spanish column evacuating *Cascorra*, 63–69; lays siege to *Guaimaro*, assisted by Calixto Garcia, 70–81; 125; 149.
*Guaimaro*, siege of, 74–81.
*Guerrilleros*, Cubans loyal to Spain, 83–84; 101; 108; 109; *insurrectos* wreak vengeance upon, 118.
*Guisa*, 128.
*Hartley & Graham*, arms dealers, 23.
*Holguin*, 110.
Honolulu, Hawaii, 4–5.
Hotchkiss guns, 23; 27; 57; 60; 75; 79; 104–105; 111; 127.